D1479391

T H E
NURTURING
P A R E N T

HOW TO
RAISE
CREATIVE,
LOVING,
RESPONSIBLE
CHILDREN

John S. Dacey, Ph.D.
Alex J. Packer, Ph.D.

A FIRESIDE BOOK
A Division of Simon & Schuster
New York   London   Toronto
Sydney   Tokyo   Singapore

FIRESIDE
Simon & Schuster Building
Rockefeller Center
1230 Avenue of the Americas
New York, New York 10020

Copyright © 1992 by John S. Dacey, Ph.D. and Alex J.
Packer, Ph.D.

FIRESIDE and colophon are registered trademarks of
Simon & Schuster Inc.
Designed by Pei Loi Koay
Manufactured in the United States of America

10 9 8 7 6 5 4 3 2 1

Library of Congress Cataloging-in-Publication Data

Dacey, John S.
The nurturing parent: how to raise creative,
loving, responsible children/John Dacey, Alex Packer.
p.   cm.
"A Fireside book."
Includes bibliographical references and index.
1. Parenting—United States.   2. Parents—United States—
Attitudes.   3. Creative ability in children—United States.
4. Responsibility.   I. Packer, Alex J., 1951–   .   II.
Title.
HQ755.83.D33   1992
649'.1—dc20   92-14713
                                                CIP

ISBN 0-671-77145-0

To Michael and Rekha

and to the late Dwight Lounsbery,

this book is lovingly dedicated.

CONTENTS

ACKNOWLEDGMENTS

Most books that are based on extensive research are the results of the efforts of many people. This book is no exception. If we were to try to list all those who have contributed, we would surely leave someone out.

Instead, we want to thank those who have contributed directly to this volume. We are grateful for the help of Dr. Theresa Fitzpatrick, Daniel Harrell, Tracy Hurd, Kathleen Lennon, Karen Maquire, Deborah Margolis and Elizabeth Renick, all of whom are or have been students at Boston College. We certainly appreciate the fine advice we have had from our agent, Gail Ross, and our two editors, Toni Sciarra and Sheridan Hay. Dr. Linda Schulman read the manuscript completely and gave us many fine suggestions. We would not have finished without the help we received from Ann Donaruma in guiding this book to completion.

And last, and in some ways most, we want to say how much we appreciate the fantastic cooperation we got from all the members of all the families who participated in our study.

1

NURTURING
PARENTING

*O*ur discovery of a wonderful new way of parenting was accidental.

It all began with a group of extraordinary children. We had set out to investigate the causes of creativity—specifically those factors in the family and home that produce highly creative kids. In the course of our research, our team of psychologists and educators spent over 1,400 hours interviewing highly creative kids and their families. We expected, based on the stereotype, that many of these children would be unreliable and self-involved, reclusive and "strange." To our great surprise, we found nothing of the sort! Virtually without exception, these super-creative kids were super in general: responsible, articulate, and socially adept. They possessed wit, insight, and motivation. They were ethical and empathetic, confident and caring. They were popular with their schoolmates and worked hard at household chores and part-time jobs. In the company of their parents they were relaxed and respectful, yet when the intellectual gauntlet was thrown, they rose to the challenge with exuberance.

It seemed too good to be true. We kept looking for the catch.

"I guess your children must have a hard time in school," we said at one of the group sessions we held with parents. "Being so creative and all?"

"Not at all," the parents replied.

"They tend to be loners, though?"

"I wish!" one mother said.

"Well, are they moody? Volatile?"

"I think my son is very sensitive to his emotions," one of the fathers said thoughtfully, "but he's not emotionally sensitive. If you know what I mean." The other parents seemed to know exactly what he meant. "If he's deep in some mood, it's something he wants to figure out. But he doesn't let it tear him up."

Was this, at long last, the perfect child? (No, their rooms were still messy.) But clearly something special was going on.

"How on earth have you done it?" we asked the parents. We pressed question after question, asking about rules, bedtimes, schools, and curfews. The parents responded to our questions with modesty and good humor—but their opinions were strong, and their values well-defined. The more we listened the more we heard the same story—a story of parents who trusted and respected their children, who truly enjoyed their company. Of parents who imposed few, if any, rules, yet who had no problems with discipline. Of parents who exerted little pressure to achieve, yet who looked with pride on their children's achievements.

As they described their philosophy of child-raising, the second big surprise of our study was brought to light: although none of the parents in our study knew each other, the methods and attitudes they described were amazingly similar. We could come to only one conclusion: *this approach to child-raising, strikingly missing in parenting literature, was responsible for creating these marvelously capable and creative kids.*

We call parents who espouse this style of child-raising "nurturing parents." We think theirs is the best way to raise children—as well as the way to raise the best children!

A warning is necessary, though. Nurturing parenting is not for parents who place the highest premium on obedience, neatness, and docility, or for parents who prefer their children's lives to be highly structured—with interests chosen, goals planned, and deadlines set. It is not for parents who believe that kids should always fit in, toe the line, respect authority, and reach unquestioningly for safe answers, good grades, and gold stars.

Nurturing parenting *is* for parents who want, above all, to raise healthy children—children who tackle life with humor and enthusiasm, who are flexible, joyful, independent, and self-motivating, who can embrace change, delay gratification, and think imaginatively. We believe these are the children who will have the best chance for success and happiness in today's world. These are the children we came to know through our research.

THE CREATIVITY STUDY THAT LED TO THE DISCOVERY OF THE NURTURING PARENT

When we began our four-year study of highly creative children in the mid-1980s, we hoped to learn more about how highly creative adolescents got to be that way. Our interest in this area was a natural outgrowth of our backgrounds in education and psychology, and our long-standing interest in creativity and creative approaches to learning.

John Dacey earned his Ph.D. in Educational Psychology from Cornell University. He is Professor and Chairman of the Developmental and Educational Psychology Program at Boston College since 1968; he is the author of twenty-two articles and eight books in the field of human development and family life—among them *Fundamentals of Creative Thinking*, and "Discriminating Characteristics of the Families of Highly Creative Adolescents" in *The Journal of Creative Behavior*. He is the proud father of three creative and successful daughters.

Alex Packer was a leader of play groups and summer camps for 5-to-10-year-olds while attending Harvard College. He holds a Master's degree in Education from the Harvard Graduate School of Education, a Ph.D. in Educational and Developmental Psychology from Boston College, and was the Headmaster for eight years of an innovative school in Washington, D.C., for children 11 to 16. Alex was Director of Education for the Capital Children's Museum and is the author of *Bringing Up Parents: The Teenager's Handbook*.

Our many and varied experiences with children and parents have reinforced our belief that *most of a child's personality is learned, and that the most powerful force acting upon that personality is the parents' style of child-raising*. Much of our work up to this point had focused on the design of curricula and learning environments that foster a child's motivation and self-confidence. Now, we wanted to look more closely at the relationship between parents, home environment, and creativity.

We gathered our thirteen-member team of psychologists and faculty and students from Boston College. We then asked teachers, guidance counselors, and directors of programs for the gifted all over New England to nominate the most creative teenagers in

their school districts as subjects for our research. These nomina
tions were made not on the basis of test scores or assessments of
creative potential, but on the basis of *actual creative accomplishment*. For example, among the children were:

- a 12-year-old boy who wrote and produced a half-hour radio play;
- a 16-year-old girl who won a national competition for sculpture;
- an 18-year-old boy who won a scholarship to Harvard for
  innovative work in mathematics;
- a 13-year-old girl who choreographed and starred in a ballet
  program;
- a young man who, by age 19, had written and illustrated two
  children's books for a major publishing company.

Ultimately, fifty-six families, with one hundred children between them, participated in the study. Twenty additional families
in which no family member was highly creative were also included for purposes of comparison.

The research consisted of testing administered to the children,
followed by many hours of interviewing family members on a variety of topics concerning the family's life-style. All of the interviews
were conducted so that no family member was aware of the responses of the others. When the perceptions of family members
were later compared, they were found to be surprisingly in accord.

As a result of this study, we were able to identify a number of
factors in upbringing and home environment that appear to foster
high creative ability in children. These elements are discussed
throughout this book. As we pored over our research findings, we
were astonished by the consistency of the children's attributes and
the parents' attitudes and methods. As researchers, we were skep-
tical of this consistency. Why should a random group of highly
creative kids turn out to be so similar to one another in personality and character traits? It seemed incredible that almost none of
these children would be depressed, rebellious, socially awkward,
or at loggerheads with their parents. It seemed even more unlikely that we could choose our subjects so independently, yet
find such a unanimity of values and child-raising methods—unless
the children initially shared something in common besides their

creativity. We came to the conclusion that this was the case. With similar "products"—healthy, outgoing, achieving kids who also, as it happened, were highly creative—it made sense that the "manufacturing process"—parenting methods—would be similar as well. Given the fact that these kids were unlike most of their peers, it made sense that the methods practiced by their parents would bear little resemblance to any of the other three recognized styles of child-raising.

THE THREE OTHER *WAYS TO RAISE CHILDREN*

On the basis of an extensive review of the literature, psychologist Diana Baumrind has identified three distinct parenting styles: authoritarian, permissive, and authoritative.

AUTHORITARIAN PARENTING
"YOU'LL DO WHAT YOU'RE TOLD!"

Authoritarian parents strive for control over their children's behavior by establishing complex sets of rules. They enforce the rules through the use of rewards and, often, strong discipline. These households have little room for negotiation.

Children of authoritarian parents may achieve, but they may also become withdrawn and unenthusiastic, hoping to elude their parents' wrathful radar. They tend to base their opinions of themselves on what others think, and thus are vulnerable to deep feelings of rejection and guilt. Not surprisingly, these children have the most problems later in life with interpersonal relationships, since they may not have mastered the skill of negotiation and because they may have learned to suppress their needs and desires.

PERMISSIVE PARENTING
"WHATEVER YOU WANT, DEAR."

Permissive parents exert little or no control over their children's behavior. They refrain from disciplinary measures. When their

Sea of Tranquility is whipped up in the wake of events, they are able to overlook their children's transgressions with a sigh, and a handy philosophy: "I sowed some wild oats in my day, too," or "How are kids going to learn if they don't make mistakes?"

The kids aren't fooled by such facile philosophizing, however; they suffer the results of their parents' indulgence and/or indifference. They score the highest on anxiety tests and frequently express concerns about their own mental health, both apparently caused by lack of parental guidance and support. Often promiscuous, they are impulsive and aggressive. Since they have never been asked to practice responsibility and self-control, they demonstrate low levels of each.

AUTHORITATIVE PARENTING
"WE'LL SEE."

Authoritative parenting is the most common parenting style today. Well-intentioned, these parents are sometimes authoritarian, sometimes permissive, often carefully balanced in between. Their responses vary with the circumstances and, occasionally, with the mood they themselves happen to be in. In a way, they are fair-weather freedom givers. So long as behavior is to their liking, they invest their children with rights and rewards. When interests clash, however, parental authority must predominate. The child gets a vote, but the parent gets two.

The guidance authoritative parents give to their children goes a long way toward helping them to become independent and cooperative adults. These kids generally have low anxiety and high expectations for themselves. They hold positive attitudes toward education and value achievement and competence. Respecting authority, they enjoy being told what to do, and they look to others for validation of self-worth.

Children of authoritative parents are usually friendly, obedient, and well-adjusted. Within this silver lining, however, lies a cloud. In their haste to please others, some of these kids lose touch with themselves. Their identities erode as their lives take on contours mapped out by adults. Unlikely to rebel against the love-staked boundaries that keep them, these kids may never get the chance to search for the goals and values that fit them best. More and more, they tend to acquiesce to the will of those whom they respect and perceive as being powerful. As a result, it is possible for some children of authoritative parents to develop rigid, habit-bound personalities. Looking to the outside for approval, anxious to achieve, they judge themselves critically and strive for unrealistic goals. They become less flexible in their thinking, and shy away from conflict situations.

There is no question that authoritative parents care deeply about their children, and the children know it. On the strength of that, the kids generally function well out in the world. As they grow up and move through adulthood, however, they may be pursued by one nagging thought: *Gee, I wonder who I really am?*

THE FOURTH STYLE OF CHILD-RAISING

NURTURING PARENTING
"SO WHAT DO *YOU* THINK?"

Nurturing parents respect their children's autonomy, thoughts, and feelings. Rather than imposing priorities, they encourage children to find their own. They do not pressure, they support. Neither authoritarian nor permissive, they provide their children with a clear structure of values that encourages self-discipline, commitment, and intellectual and creative freedom. They differ from authoritative parents in that they tend to be more consistent in dealing with their children and more willing to let them learn through experience. They believe that children get better at the things they practice. Accordingly, they believe that children must have responsibility if they are to become responsible; that they must make their own decisions if they are to learn good judgment.

Perhaps more than anything, nurturing parents *trust*. They trust their child's fairness and judgment. This is not to say they believe that all children are born "good," bursting from the womb with their homework done and their noses clean. Rather, they trust that all children have the capacity to *become* good—to become compassionate, reliable, and motivated—as long as they have positive examples, and the freedom to develop into the people they wish themselves to be. Nurturing parents strive to be models, not molders.

Children raised by nurturing parents excel in their relationships to themselves, to others, and to the world. Their fullness as human beings rests upon a tricornered foundation:

- responsibility
- empathy
- creativity

The parents we studied believe that children who possess these three attributes will best be able to build positive self-identity (through their creativity), loving relationships (through their empathy), and a meaningful place in the world (through their responsibility).

HOW TO USE THIS BOOK

Nurturing parents do not follow a rigid set of formulas. The story of nurturing parenting is a story of forming attitudes and relationships that reflect the individual nature of each family. Once you understand the basic ideas, you can personalize them to fit your own values and your child's unique interests and needs.

In Chapter 2, "Who Is the Nurtured Child?", we look at what it is that makes children raised this way so well-equipped to tackle the world and enjoy life. In Chapter 3, "Who Is the Nurturing Parent?", we discuss in detail the methods and values which define nurturing parenting. We identify six principles practiced by all nurturing parents. They:

... TRUST their child's fairness and good judgment;
... RESPECT their child's autonomy, thoughts, and feelings;
... SUPPORT their child's interests and goals;
... ENJOY their child's company
... PROTECT their child from doing injury to self or others;

... MODEL the self-control, sensitivity, and values they believe their child will need.

For each of these principles, we present specifics. What does it mean to respect a child's autonomy? How do you get to the point where you can trust a child's good judgment? How do these concepts, which sound so clear on paper, hold up in the chaotic, unpredictable whirl of family life?

Another major finding of our study is that there are ten traits of thinking and personality that nourish the creativity, responsibility, and empathy of children we studied. We found that, consciously and subconsciously, nurturing parents foster the development of these traits:

1. functional freedom
2. stimulus freedom
3. delay of gratification
4. balanced brain
5. originality
6. androgyny
7. self-control
8. passion
9. tolerance of ambiguity
10. problem-solving

These ten traits are mutually reinforcing: a balanced brain facilitates originality, which is enhanced by androgyny which energizes problem-solving; passion is kept in check by self-control, which is supported by tolerance of ambiguity which allows delay of gratification. The nurturing of one trait strengthens the others, and the whole is greater than the sum of its parts.

Using test facsimiles, puzzles, and other exercises, we define, in Chapters 4 through 13, each of the ten traits so that parents can easily recognize and nurture them. We discuss the parental attitudes and values that underlie each trait, as well as any family issues or conflicts that might restrict its growth. Finally, we present more than one hundred activities that parents can use to foster the development of these ten traits.

We have tried to make these activities engaging, full of humor, and easy to put to use immediately. They are designed for variety and high interest, and most can be done with one or many children. They call for little if anything in the way of supplies or preparation time. All they require are adults and children who wish to enjoy each other's company.

We believe that these activities are an excellent way to build a mutually reinforcing network of family relationships between siblings, parents, grandparents, and children. When household interests and projects overlap; when one creative spirit enriches another; when each family member participates in the growth of the others, then the whole family enjoys the harmony that fosters true closeness.

No matter how loving the family, even nurturing parents must send their children to school. There, children may encounter vastly different expectations and values than those they experience at home. In Chapter 14, "The Nurturing School," we look at the relationship between education and the developing personality. Due to the maturity and originality of their thinking, the children of nurturing parents can be at high risk for becoming bored and dispirited with their schooling. With the checklists and advice we provide, parents can identify those teachers and schools that will best facilitate their children's abilities and complement the values of the home.

There is one final point we wish to make. It is natural, in an increasingly tumultuous and stressful world, for parents to want to insure that their children will come out on top. Accordingly, there are any number of books available that purport to make children smarter, to improve their grades, and to give them a leg up on the competition. Well-meaning parents can learn to apply "developmental steroids" to virtually any aspect of their children's lives and thus strive to raise a creative child; a responsible child; a self-disciplined child; a street-smart, sports-confident, cholesterol-free, PG-in-an-X-rated-world child. Valuable as these traits may be, they are merely traits—merely parts—of what should be an integrated whole.

What sets the children of nurturing parents apart is their ability to integrate the healthy personality traits described in this book, to reconcile opposites in order to solve a problem or give birth to a creative product. They are good at communicating between their conscious and unconscious minds; they move swiftly and easily between the intuitive and the analytical, between the dream and the reality. They are superior integrators of the components of self, and adept pilots of that self into the larger world.

The ability to integrate is not a specific skill, like reading, spelling, or arithmetic, that parents can focus on at an early age in order to improve a child's chances for "success." The parents we studied are adamant in their opposition to the "hurried child" syndrome and stress that the nurturing of an integrated, whole personality does not rush their children into anything—other than the delight and satisfaction that flow from increased competence, confidence, and creativity.

To encourage a child in these directions is to encourage the growth of a vital inner life—to push, not for grades and conformity and miniature adulthood, but for play and joy, for passion and open-mindedness—so that *the child within* may keep on living into a merry old age. That is how the parents in our study define success—by the warmth and honesty of their children's relationships, by the depth and morality of their principles, by the dexterity and imagination of their minds. Nurturing parents hope that their children will find success in the "real world," but mostly they want their children to find it within themselves!

2

WHO IS THE
NURTURED CHILD?

*I*n his recent book, *Mis-Education: Preschoolers at Risk* (1987), Dr. David Elkind, Professor of Child Study at Tufts University, says: "Success in life is not the product of acquired academic skills; rather, success in life is the product of a healthy personality." What, exactly, made the kids in our study so healthy? Through many hours of interviews and discussions, three general attributes emerged:

Responsibility. They could be counted on. They took pride in their ability to keep a promise. They frequently could be seen accepting responsibility even in situations where no one had asked them to, and were three times more likely than their peers to abstain from drugs and alcohol.

Empathy. These children understood and cared about their fellow human beings to a degree not only remarkable for their age, but remarkable even when compared to the average adult.

Creativity. It was not surprising that this trait was so prevalent—after all, it was the characteristic used to identify these children in the first place. What was surprising, however, was the degree to which this creativity inspirited the whole of their lives.

We will refer to these three attributes throughout this book. They form the "tripod of support" upon which the healthy personality and successful child develop. Let's look more closely at these attributes and see what the parents and children in our study had to say about them.

1. RESPONSIBILITY

"Tell us what your children are really like," we said at one of the evening discussions we held with parents. We turned on the tape recorder and settled back to listen.

"Hard-working."

"Trustworthy."

"Principled."

"Purposeful."

"Self-correcting."

Regardless of the words they used, virtually all parents described their child as extraordinarily responsible:

"When she says she's going to do something, I know it'll get done."

"I have great faith in his judgment."

"If I were ever stranded in the middle of nowhere, I'd want him with me. If I sent him for help, I know he'd get it."

When asked to rate their children on thirteen traits, such as "having a high IQ" and "being popular with peers," parents consistently chose "having outstanding traits of character such as honesty and trustworthiness" as the most accurate description.

This finding was seconded by the youngsters themselves. Almost without exception, they said that they worked harder than their schoolmates, and had done so since starting school. This was not just true for schoolwork; they also felt that they worked harder than their peers at chores, jobs, and hobbies.

It was this remarkable drive and responsibility that allowed these children to function in the world and to meet the necessary obligations of life.

We found this characteristic of "doing what you say you will do" to be highly related to being creative. This finding is supported by the results of two other recent studies, one of sixth to ninth graders (Collier et al., 1987), and one of gifted secondary school students (Olzewski-Kubilius et al., 1988).

2. EMPATHY

Another set of parental reflections clustered around the traits of self-awareness and empathy:

"Very insightful."

"Compassionate. If it were up to my child, we'd be running a shelter for every stray cat and dog within two hundred miles."

"My daughter must have twenty 'best' friends. I think it's because she's very empathetic. She often tells me about her friends' latest heartbreak or family crisis or love emergency (and at that age they have about ten of them a day)."

"All during high school, my son organized and ran play groups for kids in the neighborhood twice a week after school. He'd take them on trips to the harbor, or to the control tower at the airport, or they'd play sports or make movies or go swimming. The parents were thrilled, and my son made a small fortune from it—but every now and then he'd bring them to our house, usually to cook (we have a very big kitchen; cooking is sort of a family hobby). I'd peek in to see how things were going. I'll never forget that one day, two of the kids got into a fight. You know how scared kids get when they realize they're out of control? Well, these two boys— they must have been five or six—were shaking and crying, and my son, who is six foot three and played football in high school, kneeled down to talk to them and comfort them, and I thought to myself, 'He's going to be such a wonderful mother!' The thought just hung in my head for a moment until I realized the slip. That's still one of the loveliest images I have of him. He has always had this very gentle and caring side."

Over and over, the parents in our study described children who enjoy close relationships with adults, peers, and often, much younger children, and who demonstrate great insight into the motives behind human behavior.

One father spoke of a short yet stormy period he and his wife went through with their daughter when she was fourteen. ". . . Let's just say we had different definitions of 'safe' behavior. We'd have these arguments which would get rather theatrical. Usually, however, within a day's time, after everyone had calmed down, my daughter would either ask to talk to us again or write us a note, and proceed to analyze why she had felt the way she did, or why she had said a certain thing, or she'd ascribe some hidden agenda to my wife or me, or say we were putting our own fears onto her. Her observations were uncanny in their accuracy, and nearly always paved the way to a solution. Eventually, she was able to remain calm enough during the first discussion to allow her insights to surface."

This high degree of empathy and self-awareness may have been due to the interesting fact that children in our study reported a much larger number of traumatic incidents during childhood than do other children. These were occurrences that caused grief, anger, or both, or that seriously disrupted the child's life: the deaths of parents, siblings, grandparents, or pets; divorce, moving, accidents, hospitalizations. The parents of the creative youth in our study remembered from two to nine of these incidents; parents in the comparison group of families could remember only one to three such occasions. Although it is possible that the former group may simply be more sensitive to pain and loss, and thus remembered more of these incidents, several theorists believe that dealing with childhood trauma is a major cause of creativity, particularly among writers. We should note, however, that this is not the same as saying that creative children are more emotionally disturbed than their peers. While creative kids appear to experience a greater number of emotionally disturbing events, they also seem to develop a greater capacity to deal with them successfully. They are able to integrate pain into their view of life, and arrive at deeper and ultimately more empathetic understandings of themselves and others.

This capacity to "process" their feelings may be one reason for the unexpected sociability we found in the highly creative children of our study. Their heightened empathy draws them toward other children; their peers, in turn, seek them out as supportive and desirable friends. In their own ratings of the thirteen behaviors that most accurately describe them, these kids consistently gave "getting along well with others," a high rating. The stereotype of creative children as reclusive and socially awkward was not borne out by our study.

We also found a close relationship between empathy and responsibility. Hamilton and Friegel (1988) came to the same conclusion in their study of eleven- to seventeen-year-olds. A number of other studies have lent support to the finding that parents can substantially increase their children's ability to empathize (Amato,

1989; Bernstein and Glenn, 1988; Hall, 1984; Keltikangas, 1990; Knowska, 1987; Spillane-Grielco, 1984).

Empathy and responsibility make for a powerhouse combination that allows children to connect to others in joyful and enriching ways. It is no wonder that children who possess these traits are so effective in interpersonal interactions and are able to build and maintain intimate relationships later in life.

3. CREATIVITY

The parents we studied agreed that the attributes of empathy and responsibility stood out immediately as being strongly characteristic of their children. Soon, however, a less consistent pattern emerged:

"Very inquisitive. Always wants to know *why* something is."

"He's not really interested in the input of others."

"Very open-minded."

"Once's he's made up his mind about something, you can't budge him with a bulldozer!"

"Playful."

"Serious."

"He likes to be alone. He seems to need a certain amount of time to himself."

"He's always inviting friends over to the house."

What struck us at first about these depictions was their inconsistency: these parents portrayed their children as sociable *and* solitary, open-minded *and* stubborn, dilettantish *and* focused. When we placed the template of creativity over them, however, the fit was perfect.

This is because the essence of the creative personality lies in its ability to bridge the extremes and to integrate all parts of the self—to be childlike *and* mature, flexible *and* uncompromising. Creative children are like jugglers; they seem to enjoy the disparate elements of their personality. They play with each, testing and fine-tuning, until the parts become the whole—a marvelous, spinning, interrelated whole—which is their creativity.

What more could a parent ask?

"Well, for one thing, they could be a little neater."

"You mean they're not perfect?" we asked in mock disbelief. Parents hooted. "Hardly."

What followed was a recitation of faults—sloppiness, impulsivity, disinterest in school, argumentativeness, stubbornness.

But unlike other discussions of child-rearing problems that we've had with parents in which anger and frustration fill the air, this discussion was light—full of humor and acceptance. Parents saw their children's annoying characteristics as the flip side of their endearing ones.

"I have always told my children to think for themselves and to stand up for their principles. Of course, it can be a little galling when they turn this advice around in the middle of an argument and use it against you."

"Sometimes my daughter and I get into rather animated discussions over some issue, and although I'm pleased we're communicating, at the same time my blood pressure is rising and it takes every ounce of self-control I have to keep from saying, 'Because I said so, dammit! That's why!!' "

"I find that my children are tremendously self-controlled in areas that interest them, including homework, but when they don't care, dynamite couldn't move them. Cleaning their bedrooms is a good example."

"My very creative daughter insists on wearing the most outlandish clothes—never anything that's in style. Once I said to her, 'Have you any idea what people must be thinking of you?' and she said, 'That doesn't matter—I want to *set* the trends.' "

Most of the personality traits demonstrated by the adolescents in our study are delightful to behold: perseverance, playfulness, curiosity, resourcefulness. Others are more challenging to parental serenity: risk-taking, heightened emotional sensitivity, eagerness to question the status quo. The boundless curiosity that leads to discovery and growth can also lead to times when even the most patient parent will be tempted to shout, "Don't ask so many questions!" The risk-taking that leads to new skills and experiences can also lead to broken bones and expensive mistakes. Where is the line between reasonable risk-taking and recklessness? When does perseverance become pigheadedness?

One parent was concerned that her son's great interest in everything could lead to a lack of achievement in anything. "He seems to resonate to every little thing that goes on around him, so much so that he cannot concentrate on any one thing for very long. He has wonderful reactions, but never follows through on any of them."

Other parents assured her that this is typical of highly creative children. "They're samplers. They want to try everything. But they grow out of it. Or maybe I should say, they add to it, so that as they get older, their self-discipline increases, and they're able to pursue things for a longer amount of time. But I think creative people are always interested in lots of things."

A father voiced a related concern. "Many creative children seem to be very impulsive. They get so excited about something that they rush into it without thinking. Naturally we try to caution them, but I think we really should be careful about killing that wild enthusiasm."

"Isn't that the point of being a parent?" one father remarked. "To show—and I emphasize show as opposed to tell—where those lines and limits are? Where constructive becomes destructive?"

"I'm an architect," he continued. "When I start a new project, I race from idea to idea, I've got sketches on napkins, placemats, book margins. I'll pursue ideas madly, then drop them cold. My kids see me being impulsive. And disordered. But sooner or later, they also see me focused, neat, and obsessed with details. They know that one extreme without the other is useless.

"But should I presume to control my child's creative process? To know whether he's being impulsive or gathering information? What might look like an inability to follow through now, could really be critical to some larger process later. It keeps coming back to trust."

Like almost all parents in our study, this father *trusted his son's creative process*. "I remember as a kid, getting into more than my fair share of trouble. Never mundane trouble, but what I'd call creative trouble, principled trouble. Things like picketing, organizing protests, printing articles in the school paper that caused the administration to have a collective cow. Recently I visited my parents and we were reminiscing and I asked them if I had caused them a lot of worry as a child. 'Of course we worried,' they said. 'But no matter what trouble you got yourself into, you always seemed to land on your feet.' That's what I mean when I say I trust my kid. He always seems to land on his feet. Frankly, I'd rather have a kid I know can land on his feet than a kid who never gets off balance in the first place!"

Virtually all parents in our study saw their children as "being different." In the case of our architect father, it was his son's feline powers of balance; for other parents it was their child's maturity or depth of feeling that set them apart. The children also regarded themselves as "being different," and said they remembered thinking so at an early age. Most felt that this had been an asset:

"My friends respect me for being different from them."

"Sometimes I think I would absolutely totally die of boredom if I had to be like most kids in my school."

Their rooms were different, too—overstuffed with their owners' expressiveness. In one room, representative of many, every square inch of wall space was covered with books, posters, or postcards; there was an antique pogo stick in one corner and a nude store mannequin with rubber insects crawling over it in another. The desk carried a computer, three-foot-high stacks of magazines, and pads of paper with various incarnations of a sketch. Above the desk was a framed, hand-lettered sign: "I Never Let My Schooling Interfere With My Education." Thumb-tacked to the frame were prize ribbons: Lincoln Junior High Spelling Bee—1st Place; 4-H Club 2nd Prize (for summer squash, we learned); World's Greatest Person Grand Prize Winner (obviously a home-made award!). Several clotheslines crisscrossed the room, dangling an awesome array of photographs, reminder notes, articles of clothing, and cooked linguine (the occupant was interested in seeing how long linguine would last in the natural environment).

The rooms of these children, like their inhabitants, were full of wit, irony, and individuality. Everyday objects were given new twists: mannequins wearing insects, pole lamps wearing clothing, floors painted with clouds. It is no surprise to discover that these kids, in choosing from that list of thirteen behaviors mentioned earlier, most often ranked "best able to look at things in a new way and discover new ideas" number one. What a wonderful image to have of oneself!

We had wondered if there were gender differences in creative ability; certainly, male creativity has received more recognition historically than that of females. In our study, fathers had significantly higher creativity scores than mothers in almost all categories. However, we found the male and female youth to be about equal in their creativity ratings. This finding could be explained by the narrow role definitions which limited women at the time these mothers were growing up; now that options for females have increased, so too have their creativity scores. No doubt women have always had as much creative ability as men; it's just that female creativity, until recently, was usually sacrificed on the altar of "ladylike" behavior.

PUTTING IT ALL TOGETHER

Creativity lies at the heart of the child raised in a nurturing home. But creativity, no matter how glorious and inspiring, is not enough to insure that a child will lead a rich, well-balanced life. It is possible for children to be creative yet irresponsible, creative yet uncaring about others. They may use their creativity to escape life rather than embrace it.

In order to be a positive force in a child's life, creativity must walk arm in arm with responsibility and empathy. It is this linkage that nurturing parents forge: in the structures they provide, the questions they ask, the answers they give; in the values they set, the choices they offer, the passions they model. How, exactly, do these parents do it? What is their philosophy? What are their methods? In the next chapter we begin to answer these questions.

3

WHO IS THE NURTURING PARENT?

*C*onsider the following school psychologist's report:

> *Tommy is an intelligent, unkempt child in poor physical health due to frequent bouts with viral infection. His teachers report that the quality of his schoolwork is generally low, and that he has great difficulty with spelling and rote learning. He shows little interest in reading or writing and manifests a consistently negative attitude toward school in general. He frequently interrupts classes by "asking foolish questions," being rude to teachers, and playing practical jokes on others.*
>
> *Recently, he set fire to a portion of his home, and when asked why, replied, "Because I wanted to see what the flames would do." The boy was given a public beating by his father, in full view of the neighborhood. He has attempted to hatch chicken eggs by sitting on them, and when this didn't work, he encouraged his playmates to swallow some raw. Neighbors frequently note explosions coming from the basement of the boy's home, where his mother permits him to play with chemical substances.*
>
> *Tommy's father has little regard for his son's intelligence, and states that strong disciplinary intervention and obedience training are the best methods for dealing with the boy. Nevertheless, Tommy's mother, a former schoolteacher, insists that he be withdrawn from school and allowed to stay at home and receive the rest of his education from her.*
>
> *In light of the boy's repeated failures in school, his resolutely negative attitude, and his social maladaptation to the*

peer group, home tutoring may be a viable alternative to the current situation. It should be noted, however, that the abusive behavior of the father, as well as the conflict between the parents, may be exacerbated by the boy's spending an increased amount of time in the home environment. This would, of course, be of considerable detriment to Tommy's development.

Tommy's mother did take her son out of school, and the boy's creativity flourished. Nevertheless, even she must have been surprised by the degree of her son's success when Thomas went on to change the world with his invention of the light bulb and the phonograph!

History leaves no doubt as to Thomas Alva Edison's extraordinary creativity. Clearly, his mother's support protected and nurtured it. But his parents' arguments, his social isolation, and the shame and abuse he suffered at the hands of his father caused lasting scars. As an adult, Edison was difficult to work with and uncomfortable in his personal relationships. His marriage was unhappy. Edison's creativity, like the filaments in a light bulb, shone in a vacuum. It was not integrated into the larger world—into his relationships, his self-esteem. As our fictionalized school psychologist predicted, Edison's family life did cause lasting damage to his personal development.

Unlike Edison's parents, who were alternately authoritarian (public beatings) and permissive (explosions in the basement?!?), the parents in our study promoted their children's well-being in a stable context. They not only nurtured their child's creativity, they nurtured the whole child. They did this by following six fundamental principles that form the heart of nurturing parenting. These principles are not static beliefs. On the contrary, they are active forces which these parents use to shape their relationships with their children, and their children's relationships to the world. Let's examine them here:

1. NURTURING PARENTS **TRUST**
. . . THEIR CHILDREN'S FAIRNESS
AND GOOD JUDGMENT.

Nothing is more central to the concept of nurturing parenting than trust. Parents in our study stated over and over again how much they trusted their child's judgment and decency. "I believe in the goodness of children," one father remarked.

"I don't think anyone here is saying that children raised in a vacuum of parental attention will be good," he replied when we asked him to clarify. "What we're saying is that *children will be good if they see goodness, if they live with goodness, and, this is most important, if they are allowed to choose their own form of goodness.*"

The concept of choosing one's own course of goodness is not new. For example, "doing your own [good] thing" was expressed as an educational philosophy in the "free" schools which prospered during the late 1960s and early '70s. It was believed that by placing children in an unstructured environment, they would naturally become motivated, self-disciplined, and hard-working. But sadly, what happened to many children was just the reverse. With no rules and no requirements, they became stuck. They didn't grow or know what else they could do because they didn't know what else was out there.

The schools begun in that era that still thrive are, by and large, the schools that believe that children need and want to be challenged. Likewise, the parents in our study defined trust as an *activity*, not just an attitude. "You have to show kids how to be trustworthy. They have to know what it is that makes you trust them, so that they can cultivate and trust those things in themselves."

Before trust can exist, a child has to know what his or her parents mean by good judgment or moral behavior. Nurturing parents trust their children's fairness because they themselves have demonstrated fairness. They trust their children's judgment because they have shown them how to make good decisions. They trust their children's morals because they have raised them in a household with high moral principles. Children then need to *practice* those skills. Nurturing parents help their children practice by allowing them to make decisions and assume responsibility as they mature.

"Of course kids are going to make some silly or ill-advised choices," one mother said. "But that's how they learn. I'll step in if I think my child is truly going to be hurt or hurt someone else by an action. But otherwise, I think it's a lot better for him to find his own way. My son *wants* to make good decisions. So he looks hard for what is right."

Another mother observed, "Once children have done time in school, they seem to develop this dread of making mistakes. I guess they associate mistakes with failing. I've tried very consciously to counter that attitude because I think it's such a suffocating presence. Sure, mistakes can be stupid and careless, but they can also be valuable and enlightening. I tell my kids that every mistake brings them that much closer to a solution. I think that's one reason my kids come to me when they have a problem."

One father stressed that trust between parents and children can be unintentionally broken—through misunderstandings, poorly communicated expectations, missed cues, or false assumptions. He saw these causes as being sharply different from more willful breaches of trust such as lying, breaking promises, or behaving irresponsibly.

"This was brought home to me several years ago when my daughter was sixteen. I got a call from her school one day informing me that she had left school sometime during the morning. Now, I usually trusted her, yet my first thought was, '*Why, you little sneak, skipping school like that.*' Then I considered various other possibilities: that she'd been kidnapped or had run away.

"It turned out that a friend of hers had received a call telling her that her brother had just been killed in an automobile accident—it was very tragic the way it happened—I don't know how they could tell a kid something like that over the phone. This girl became quite hysterical and ran out of the school. My daughter went after her and spent the rest of the day taking care of her, trying to calm her down, getting her home, talking. That was why she had left school.

"After I understood the situation, I felt proud of her. She made exactly the sort of choice I would hope a child of mine would make. Yet, I felt ashamed of myself for making an unfair assumption about her behavior. Later, when she and I talked about it, I asked her why she hadn't called me when she must have known I would have been worried. Well, never having skipped school before, she didn't know that the school would try to reach her parents. So even there, I assumed that she had knowingly made a decision not to call. You see? Unless you know what goes through your child's mind, how can you build trust?"

Most children are eager communicators when young; whether they continue to be so as they grow older depends on the response their communications receive. Nurturing parents follow a number of principles in maintaining open, trust-building communications with their children:

• Recognize that children are entitled to their private thoughts. Don't pry. It is natural for parents to feel left out and, at times, even a bit jealous of the intense confidences children share with their peers. However, this is a situation where an indirect approach works best. If your child feels that you respect her right to emotional and intellectual privacy, she will be more likely to entrust you with her feelings and thoughts.

• Don't criticize or judge your child's attitudes, beliefs, and values. Nothing shuts up a kid faster than an adult who tramples his ideas. Would *you* reveal your hopes and concerns to someone who consistently told you what was wrong with them? A child's communications should be received as one would a gift—with tact and gratitude—even on those occasions when the "gift" is ill-chosen or other than what one had hoped for.

• Listen for the hidden messages behind your child's words. For example, your fourth grader comes home from school and announces: "I'm never going back to that stinky school again!" Some parents might respond by saying, "Don't be silly. Of course you have to go to school." This misses the point of the child's words, and threatens to turn the discussion into a power struggle: "You're going to school!" "No I'm not!" Nurturing parents would respond to this sort of comment in a different way: "You're never going back to school again? Something bad must have happened today. Tell me about it."

Look for the feelings behind your child's communications. When children say things that are selfish, vengeful, or thoughtless, it often means there's something powerful and upsetting going on beneath the surface. Don't be baited into an argument or judgmental reaction. Respond to the emotions, not the words.

Suppose your son unleashes a hurtful tirade: "I hate you! I wish you were dead! If Dad were here everything would be different—no wonder he left!" It would be natural for a parent hearing this stinging attack to hook into the *words* and respond: "How dare you talk to me that way! I'm your mother. Don't you ever say anything like that to me again. Go to your room this instant!" While such a response might reestablish temporary authority, it does nothing to further communication and understanding. A nurturing parent would reply: "You must be very angry, since it's not like you to hurt my feelings. Tell me what it is that's bothering you." This mother knows that her child's angry words are merely clues to some underlying emotional turbulence. By orienting the discussion around her son's feelings, she learns more about him, models empathy and understanding, and helps him to see the hurtful nature of his remarks. This is the sort of response that builds closeness and communication.

• Avoid the temptation to offer your child a "quick fix." It's natural for parents to want to solve their children's woes. Unfortunately, magical solutions usually don't exist. Children are much more comforted by empathy and commiseration than by artificial salves for their troubles. Avoid these easy outs that dismiss the intensity of a child's feelings:

"You'll get over it."

"I'm sure she didn't mean it."

"There'll be another chance next year."

These comments may well be true, but they're not what a child needs to hear. Nurturing parents support their children's feelings:

"No wonder you're so disappointed."

"That must have been very embarrassing."

"Sounds like it really hurt your feelings."

This emotional acknowledgment leads the child to realize that he *will* get over it, that she *didn't* mean it, and, that indeed, there *will* be another chance next year.

• Encourage communication by using the skills of *reflective listening*:

1. Rephrase your child's comments to show that you understand:

    "You feel the teacher was unfair."

    "You're afraid they'll laugh if you say you don't want to go."

    This not only fosters conversation, but allows your child to correct any misimpressions you may have received.

2. Rephrase your child's comments into statements that are less self-destructive and more suggestive of the possibility of change:

    Your child says: "Everybody hates me!"

    The nurturing parent says: "You'd like to have more friends."

    Your child says: "I can't ever do anything right!" The nurturing parent says: "It seems no matter how hard you try, something goes wrong."

3. Give nonverbal support as you listen to what your child says: a smile, a hug, a wink, a pat on the shoulder. Nod your head. Make eye contact.

4. Watch your child's face and body language. He may tell you that he isn't sad, but a quivering chin or moist eyes will tell you otherwise. She may insist through clenched chin and tapping foot that she's not angry. When words and body language say two different things, always believe the body language.

These attitudes and communication techniques build the type of family environment in which trust is most likely to flourish. When they feel that they are trusted, kids are motivated to behave responsibly and empathically. This makes it easy for parents to follow the second fundamental principal of nurturing parenting: respect.

2. NURTURING PARENTS **RESPECT**
... THEIR CHILDREN'S AUTONOMY,
THOUGHTS, AND FEELINGS.

Your children are not your children.
They are the sons and daughters of Life's longing for itself.
They come through you but not from you,
And though they are with you, they belong not to you.
You may give them your love but not your thoughts.
For they have their own thoughts.
You may house their bodies but not their souls,
For their souls dwell in the house of tomorrow, which you cannot visit, not even in your dreams...

Kahlil Gibran

The parents in our study respect their children's autonomy. They do not live through their children. You are unlikely to hear them say, "Make me proud of you." They are already proud of their children. What they want is for their children to be proud of themselves: "Do what will make *you* feel proud."

Nurturing parents respect their children's feelings. "I used to hate it," one parent remarked, "when my parents would say that something was just a stage I was going through. It was as if nothing I felt really mattered."

Another parent agreed. "When I was a kid, I was very open with my parents. But often when I told them how I felt about something they'd say, 'How can you possibly feel that way?' As I got older, I decided that my feelings must be wrong and I learned pretty quickly to keep them to myself."

Feelings are subjective, sometimes irrational, and always changeable. We cannot expect the emotional responses of a twelve-year-old to be the same as those of a forty-year-old, nor would we want them to be. It's important to listen to a child's feelings with concern and support, communicating trust in her ability to work things out. Ask questions—not to lead a child to your point of view—but to help her find her own.

"It is not my child's job to please me." This is how one mother summed up her attitude. "I don't have to live within my daughter's body, her conscience, her social network. What right do I have to expect her to feel things the way I do, or to ask her to make decisions based upon my friends, or my preferences? Or even my experience? I'm pleased when she is pleased. This assumes, of course, that I have been successful in establishing a sense of our family's values."

Respecting a child's autonomy also means that the child is responsible for his mistakes. Mistakes do not reflect upon the parent, they reflect upon the child. You can see this difference exemplified in how two parents would react to the same situation. For example, upon learning that her child had done something foolish, an authoritarian parent might say: "Oh, I'm so mortified. How could he do that? What will people think?"

A nurturing parent is likely to say: "I'm sorry my child did that. He's learning and he obviously made a serious mistake. But I'm sure he'll do whatever is necessary to set things right."

While this "hands-off" approach is often the best way for parents to foster growth and respect their children's competence, it doesn't mean that nurturing parents leave their children dangling in the wind. Sometimes, respect is best expressed not by backing off, but by jumping aboard. At these times, nurturing parents put into practice the third fundamental principle: support.

3. NURTURING PARENTS **SUPPORT**
. . . THEIR CHILDREN'S INTEREST AND GOALS.

Support is an elusive concept. It sounds marvelous when discussed as a theory, but when you translate the concept to the real world, and to the real child, just what does it mean?

Surely, support means giving your child a lot of praise, right? Wrong!! As the parents in our study put it:

"The worst thing you can do is praise your children."

"Nothing destroys creativity faster than praise."

These words fly in the face of common sense and parental instinct. How can praise possibly hurt a child? Everyone likes to hear praise. And that, in a nutshell, is the problem. The desire to hear praise leads kids *to seek it above all else*. What others think becomes more important than what they think. As one mother put it, "Praising kids makes them think that you are the real judge, so they never learn to judge their own work objectively." When this happens, motivation becomes extrinsic—work is done for the applause of others. With applause as the goal, creativity withers.

If the approval of others were a requisite for creative achievement, the world would be without some of its greatest art and inventions. To triumph over the derision or skepticism of others, it is necessary to have a highly developed sense of autonomy, and a belief in the intrinsic value of one's work. Supportive parents generate this self-sufficiency in their children.

There's another reason why praise is generally harmful, and that's because it can backfire. One father expressed it quite well:

"Some people think that the way to get productivity out of kids is to praise them. In our family, we don't do that to each other much. Several times when I've done it, my kids found out from someone else that what he or she had done was not so good, and they trusted me less. My kids really want honest criticisms of their work, not praise. Most of the time, saying something like, 'Gee, that's incredible,' amounts to baby talk, and they know it."

We aren't saying that you should criticize your children. What you should do is get children to tell you what *they* think. That will further their creativity, foster their sense of responsibility, and fine-tune their empathy. They will work to please themselves. Their motivation will be intrinsic.

This notion of withholding praise to encourage autonomy may feel very uncomfortable at first. Let's say that your child comes to you with a painting. "Do you think I got this right, Mommy?" Your immediate reaction will be to say, "I think it's just beautiful!" Try to resist this temptation. It is far better to say enthusiastically, "Let's talk about it!" Help her discover what *she* thinks "getting it right" means. What were her intentions? Was it a study of blue tones, or an attempt to depict a stormy sea? Whether she bubbles enthusiastically or looks at you blankly, she will eventually form her own opinion. She may even lose interest in yours! At that point, it is fine to tell her what you think. But even then, it is much better to ask questions and to encourage her to look deeply into her work and intentions. Praise her *effort*. "You must have worked hard on this!" "I bet it feels wonderful to be finished."

What if, when you ask your daughter what *she* thinks, she replies, "But I want to know what *you* think, Mommy." Then you need to explain that what other people think isn't as important as what *she* thinks.

This caution against praise doesn't mean parents should become nonreactive lumps of clay. Particularly as a child gets older and demonstrates intrinsic motivation, it's fine to offer reactions and criticisms—*after* she's expressed her own. With her own opinions intact, she is better able to value yours for their honesty and illumination. Your comments should still be informed by what she has told you about the purposes of her creation. Respond to *her* intentions. This is what makes for constructive criticism:

"If you want us to feel sorry for the bully in the story, I think it would be good to tell us more about him. Maybe you could add some of his thoughts, or things that happened to him when he was little."

"I have a hard time figuring out what's going on in this corner of your drawing. Is it important to your picture? Did you make it this small for a reason?"

"I see in your design that you put the parents' study right next to the family room. Do you think the noise from kids playing will make it hard for the parents to work?"

Criticism in the form of questions encourages kids to think and to challenge your interpretations of their work. You may learn that the study has been placed next to the family room so that the parents can keep an eye on the children (through a one-way mirror in the wall which, you are told, is soundproof!).

There are times when it's fine to praise children. Praise is appropriate when you are so absolutely sure of your child's feelings that the question he or she asks of you is practically rhetorical. When a 5-year-old, after weeks of mustering up the courage, takes that first triumphant leap off a diving board, and then, with water dripping from the corners of a grinning mouth, asks, "How was that?", you can exclaim, "That was great!" When, after spending three days in front of the mirror preparing for a dance, a teenager emerges from the bedroom reeking of pride if not perfume, and asks, "How do I look?", you say, "You look mah-velous, dahling!" And praise is especially needed when your child has taken an enormous risk in, for example, expressing his feelings, and has that look on his face that says he's afraid he's made a fool of himself!

Rewards can be just as damaging to autonomy as praise. Psychologist Teresa Amabile's (1989) research on creativity has shown that children who are rewarded for work tend to become less creative and motivated in the work they do. In fact, artists and writers often speak of the destructive power of financial reward and public recognition. While it is tempting to say, "We should all have such problems," one can see how it would be difficult to set off in new and risky directions when you know that the public is clamoring for more of your dot paintings at $100,000 a pop!

This phenomenon is nowhere more evident than in school, where the joyful process of learning can be mutated into the less-than-joyful pursuit of reward. A grade-schooler works, not for enjoyment and empowerment, but for a moronic smiley face. When kids look no further than the grade on a returned paper, they confirm that the reward has become the goal. When they raise their hands to ask, "Do we have to know this?", they really want to know if the reward system is in operation. If it is not, chances are, neither is their attention.

This being said, the world, and certainly parents, must depend upon such systems. How can we get children to eat without the reward of dessert to coax them through dinner? Somehow, spinach just isn't intrinsically motivating. There are days when only the reward of a paycheck gets us to face our job. In fact, why should anyone work hard if they're not going to get something out of it?

They shouldn't, and no child is going to be harmed by an *occasional* treat to underscore certain positive behaviors: taking greater responsibility for chores, better effort on homework, the cessation of nail-biting. In these situations, rewards are used as "jump starts" to bypass depleted reservoirs of motivation and recharge confidence. Parents who elect to use rewards in this fashion must wean their children from them as soon as possible. This can be done by focusing a child's attention on the *natural* benefits of her behavior: more choices, more friends, more freedom; less anxiety, less conflict, less guilt. Point the child toward the rewards that come from within—a profound satisfaction, a sense of purpose, a torrent of exhilaration.

Parents can also minimize the use of external rewards by encouraging children to reward themselves. When your child faces a daunting task, suggest that she think up some treat or incentive to help her meet the challenge. This puts the entire system of reinforcement under your child's control, which is much healthier. After all, don't most of us reward ourselves—with a dinner out, a new CD, a vacation—to get through those less-than-intrinsically-motivating times?

When a reward is indistinguishable from encouragement, it is a healthy reward. It is the difference between paying a child to practice violin every day, and supporting a child's musical dedication with the resources available to parents. Providing resources acknowledges effort, diligence, and progress, rather than product. Nurturing parents hang their children's artwork throughout the house, listen to them practice their music, and send their stories to Grandma. They provide lessons, tools, equipment, and opportunities.

But don't you sometimes *have* to force children to try something so they can see if they like it? Where are the boundaries between encouraging and forcing a child to perform?

When we raised this topic with nurturing parents and their children, the response was unanimous: so long as safety is not at stake, force plays no role in the nurturing family.

"My son is alive with interests. Why on earth should I force him in a direction he doesn't want to go?"

"Having to finish everything you start—you know, persistence for its own sake—is highly overrated in my book. Think of all the trouble people get into because they're too pigheaded to change directions or stop what their doing."

"How do *you* feel when you're forced to do something?"

"Sometimes my parents use *persuasion* on me," said one of the teenagers in our study. "You know, they tell me to give something more time, or that my expectations are off, or they suggest reasons why continuing might benefit *me*. But they never force me to do anything. I think that's why I usually take their advice—because I know I don't have to. I mean, if *they* know they're not going to force me, and *I* know they're not going to force me, why would they bother to say anything unless they really believe it?"

Nurturing parents know that when kids are motivated to learn, they are willing to endure all manner of hardship along the way. Think of the scrapes and bruises of learning to ride a bike, the numbed fingers and wet feet of learning to ski, the dented egos and broken hearts of learning to love.

"I just want to add one thing," remarked a parent as we were finishing our discussion of this issue. "If I were to say to my friends, 'I never force my kids to do anything,' they'd think I was crazy. And it does sound crazy if you isolate this question from everything else we've talked about. I don't force my kids, because *I don't have to*. I don't have to, because I trust them. They've demonstrated that they have good judgment and perseverance. And whenever I might be tempted to 'force' them, we've always been able to talk things over. It's part of a whole system. It works because of all the other things we've talked about."

4. NURTURING PARENTS **ENJOY**
. . . THEIR CHILDREN'S COMPANY.

"Encourage your kids to ask questions."

"Find out what *they* think."

"Invite them to join in some of *your* activities."

As the parents in our study described their methods, we began to wonder, isn't all of this talking and probing and explaining and questioning a rather time-intensive way to raise children?

"Well," joked one of the fathers, "I suppose tyranny is a lot more efficient than democracy, if that's what you're asking."

A mother said, "A stitch in time saves nine. That's how I see what we're doing. From day one, we give our kids good and regular servicing. Preventative maintenance, if you will. And as a result, we don't have to send our kids in for painful and expensive overhauls. If you ask me, that's cost effective."

"I'd second that," added another parent. "I have never had to spend one minute in a teacher's or principal's office to discuss a problem, my children have never gotten into trouble with the law, and we've never had what my computer programmer neighbor calls 'down-time' with our children, where they disappear for days or longer into funks or hostility and you stay up nights worrying yourself sick about them."

In discussion after discussion, we realized the common thread: these parents enjoy their kids. As families, they spend time together working on various projects, planning, dreaming, traveling. Of course, this is easier said than done in today's two-career or single-parent families. It can be difficult to coordinate parents' and kids' schedules to provide for this type of sharing. A little ingenuity, however, goes a long way toward keeping relationships close:

• Call your child from work for a ten-minute chat. You can learn the latest news, answer any pressing questions, and show your child that you're thinking of her.

• If your child will be in bed before you get home, ask him to leave you a note or picture about something important or exciting that happened during the day. Perhaps your child finds a note from you on his pillow the next morning.

• Your children can take snapshots that keep you in touch with their lives. If you have to be out of town for several days, ask your kids to show you what they did, where they went, and how they felt. It's not only a way to stay close, but also a marvelous creative opportunity for your kids.

• Take your child to work for a day. If it's practical, let your child come to your work place after school from time to time to do homework.

• Keep a logbook in a prominent, well-trafficked spot in your house. Have everyone use it to jot down thoughts, reminders, jokes, insights, and concerns.

• If you have a hard time getting together for family dinners, get together for dessert later in the evening.

The joy that nurturing families find in one another's company deepens their love. Love, of course, is the spring that feeds parental worries about their children's safety. Nurturing parents, like virtually all parents, want to protect their kids from the dangers of life. Most parents deal with these concerns by establishing rules and restrictions. Nurturing parents take a very different tack.

5. NURTURING PARENTS **PROTECT**
. . . THEIR CHILDREN FROM DOING
INJURY TO SELF OR OTHERS.

"How many rules do you have?" we asked parents and children in our study.

"Rules?"

"You know, rules for behavior—bedtimes, curfews, study hours, dating, television, where you can go, what you can do."

Parents often seemed embarrassed by the question, and some stalled for time to think of an answer. The reason soon became clear: our research revealed that these families averaged less than one rule per household! (The twenty families with no highly creative members averaged six rules.)

This dramatic finding was our first clue that a different style of parenting was afoot in these homes. Despite the absence of rules, however, these kids showed no signs of a permissive upbringing—they weren't selfish or irresponsible or directionless. In fact, they were just the opposite—giving, reliable, and motivated. It is this paradox that lies at the heart of nurturing parenting: *fewer rules make for better behavior.*

The absence of rules does not imply the absence of limits. Nurturing parents do set limits, but indirectly. The difference is vital. They communicate values, they discuss their children's behavior with them, and they certainly act to protect their children from causing injury to themselves or others. But they don't see a package of rules handed down from above as the best way to build trust and responsibility.

"The trouble with rules," one parent remarked, "is that they discourage self-discipline. Kids don't learn to control themselves."

"I learned that lesson early," said another parent. "My son, who was five or six at the time, used to drive us crazy kicking his soccer ball inside the house. So we established a rule prohibiting it. A few days later I heard a ball bouncing. I was furious and ran upstairs. My son was bouncing a basketball along the hallway. 'What are you doing?' I yelled. 'You know you're not allowed to play with balls in the house!' He began to cry. 'But you said I couldn't kick the *soccer* ball.' If he'd been older I'd have thought he was playing games with me, but he looked so surprised and injured that I suddenly realized that the whole point of having the rule had escaped him. He had just heard us say, 'No soccer ball kicking,' and he was in absolute literal compliance. From that point on we stopped making rules. Instead, we talked with him about the *reasons* for limiting behavior. We got *him* to suggest what those limits should be. This gave him a certain pride of ownership. It was no longer a question of obeying our standards. He was acting upon his own. I think that makes all the difference in the world."

Another parent added, "Discipline can become a game. You feel like you're living with a miniature defense attorney. Your kid asks if he can sleep over at a friend's and you say, 'Sure, as long as his parents are going to be home.' You find out later that the parents went out for the evening, and what does your young 'defense attorney' say? 'But, Dad, you said I could go as long as they were *going* to be home. They were home—at around midnight. I didn't know you meant that they had to be home *all* evening.' And what happens when kids meet a situation not covered by the rules? What are they going to draw on? My kids know what we value, and they've learned how to look at their actions in terms of consequences, the possible risks involved, how others might be affected. No child of mine would ever defend something he did by saying, 'But you never said I couldn't'; I don't know that I've ever ordered him not to do something. But he knows there are all sorts of things he can't do.

"What we're really talking about is getting kids to set their own standards and live up to them. I teach high-school English and one of the things I've found to be very successful is asking my students to evaluate their own work. When they turn a paper in, they have to write me a note telling me what they think of it. It's amazing how accurate their comments are, and how much this exercise improves their work over the course of the year. If they write: 'The ending's bad because the fight happens too fast and I should describe the magician more and I'm sorry my handwriting's so sloppy,' they've created a wonderful conflict for themselves: why are they turning in *this* paper if they know how to make a better one? Kids who wouldn't have been caught dead writing a second draft end up writing second and even third drafts. It gives them an amazing sense of power to know that they have this type of insight. Sometimes a student will say to me, 'But isn't that your job?' and you realize how externalized their sense of control is. The one thing you have to be careful of, though, is that kids are often much rougher on themselves than you or I would be. They assume that evaluation means criticism, and I'm forever reminding them that it also means praise. I think this self-evaluation is really the process of getting kids to establish their own rules."

It all sounded so reasonable, but... "Aren't there times," we asked, "when you have to impose your authority?"

"Sure. When the consequences of a mistake would be truly irreversible we'll put our foot down. But how many times is that really the case?"

"If your kids are used to making their own decisions, isn't it going to be difficult to get them to obey?" we asked.

"Just the reverse. They know that it's so rare for us to countermand them that they either humor us or figure there must be a good reason. And if they need to rant and rave and save a little face, so what? They're still doing what we asked."

"Let's say it's not an extreme situation, but your child wants to do something that you don't approve of. What then?"

"Then we talk. If I have concerns, I'll tell her exactly what they are, which is a good exercise for me to have to do. Sometimes I don't know exactly what it is that I object to other than the fact that I feel a general discomfort. Then I'll ask her for suggestions: how she thinks we should handle it, why she wants to do it, what she hopes to gain, etcetera. You'd be amazed at how many times you can come to a compromise—she'll call when she gets there, or do it during the day, or ask two more friends to go along, or pay for it herself, or whatever. The funny thing is, once *she's* placed in the role of finding the solution, she doesn't see it as a restriction."

"What about the mundane things, like bedtimes or curfews?" we asked.

"My children have no bedtime. They go to sleep when they're tired. If they fall asleep in school, then we have a problem, which we'll deal with. But they aren't dumb: they know that if they fall asleep during the day it's because they're staying up too late at night. So they'll give me a sheepish grin and decide to go to bed earlier. But so many wonderful things happen at night—comets, falling stars, philosophical discussions, reading in bed—how boring to go to sleep just because the clock says you should!"

"You mentioned curfews. For a while we had an eleven o'clock curfew for our daughter. When she wanted to go to a concert a hundred miles away with some friends and one of their parents, we said fine, even though she wouldn't get back until 1:00 A.M. Another night her school sponsored a star-gazing event; another time there was a midnight mass; another time we weren't able to pick her up until after 11:30. Suddenly this arbitrary curfew seemed so ridiculous. What was its point? So now we look at each thing she wishes to do separately and together we figure out a reasonable time for her to come home."

Trust, respect, discussion, compromise—these, not rules, are the elements that nurturing parents use to protect their children from harm. Nurturing parents model the values and responsibility they hope their children will develop. It is the way they live, rather than the rules they set, that maintains "discipline."

6. NURTURING PARENTS **MODEL**
. . . THE SELF-CONTROL, SENSITIVITY, AND VALUES THEY BELIEVE THEIR CHILDREN WILL NEED.

"We say to our children, do whatever you want to, but *do something*! Then we try to be good models for a highly active life."

"The best way to get your kids to work hard is to work hard. We have always had at least one family project going. We often skipped a meal because we were all into getting the project done."

Children are more likely to do what you do, not what you say. The parents in our study don't preach to their children about the values of hard work; they work hard. They don't lecture on the importance of honesty and tolerance; they try to lead honest and tolerant lives.

It's reassuring to think of the great impact of modeling on a child's learning. It means that parents do not have to be brilliant analysts of their children's psyches, they need not possess commanding overviews of educational theory; all they need to do is lead the kind of lives they hope their children will lead, be the kind of people they hope their children will be.

Often without even being aware of it, parents teach their children valuable traits and attitudes. When they change jobs and take on new challenges, they teach the value of risk-taking. When they volunteer time and donate blood, they demonstrate social responsibility; when Mother has to work late and Father comforts the baby, they teach androgyny.

The effectiveness of modeling is one reason why parents who are not themselves creative are able to raise highly creative children. Indeed, of the parents of creative children in our study, many were not themselves creative in any way. This suggests that children may well be more influenced by the quality of the environment in which they grow than by genetic inheritance.

In these first three chapters, we have explored the basic philosophy of nurturing parenting. In the next ten chapters, we sharpen our focus and examine the ten traits of thinking and personality fostered by nurturing parents that are instrumental in the development of responsibility, empathy, and creativity.

Each chapter that follows is composed of two parts. The first part describes the trait: why it's important, how it is best developed, what parental attitudes and practices foster it. The second part consists of activities, some quite simple, some more complex, that nourish and reinforce the trait. Wherever possible, we have made suggestions to keep activities stimulating across a broad age span. Parents and other caregivers will recognize that their children's individual interests and development may make some ideas more appropriate than others. We encourage the alteration of instructions and levels of difficulty. Older children often enjoy the feeling of mastery they get from doing activities targeted for younger ones, since this allows them to bring their greater sophistication and cognitive dexterity to the challenge.

Many activities can be endlessly extended by thinking up new examples, new variables, and new suppositions. As we were testing these activities, one of the most rewarding interactions we saw occurred when older brothers and sisters undertook them with younger siblings. In thinking up new activities, the older kids have to exercise the same traits they are nurturing in their younger siblings. This must explain to a large extent why we found so many of the children in the nurturing families pursuing creative endeavors.

The ten traits we describe provide a conceptual framework for understanding how nurturing parenting works. As you read the following chapters and become familiar with the traits, you will develop both a concrete and an intuitive awareness of how to encourage responsibility, creativity, and empathy in all areas of your child's life.

4

THE WHIRLING ROSARY BEADS:
FUNCTIONAL FREEDOM

A number of children were asked to suggest all the uses they could think of for a brick. One youngster volunteered, "Make a fort." Another offered, "Build a wall." A third added, "Build a house." A fourth said, "Catch worms."

"Catch worms?"

"Sure," he said. "You leave a brick on the ground, and when you come back two weeks later and pick it up, there will be worms under it!"

The child who said, "Catch worms" demonstrated *functional freedom*—the ability to see beyond the obvious, to redefine the function of an object, to discover the simple idea that solves the complicated problem. With this definition as a clue, try the following exercise (see Figure 4.1 on page 53):

You can use the clothespin or the rattrap to solve this problem by following these steps:

1. Attach either the clothespin or the rattrap to the bottom of one of the strings.
2. Swing this weighted string away from you.
3. Quickly turn and grasp the unweighted string.
4. Turn back and catch the weighted string as it swings back to you.
5. Now you may tie the ends together.

Many people are unable to reach this solution because they cannot imagine clothespins or rattraps being used for other than their usual purposes. They cannot imagine them as simple weights. This is called "functional fixity," which frequently blocks problem-solving and creative thinking. Its opposite is functional

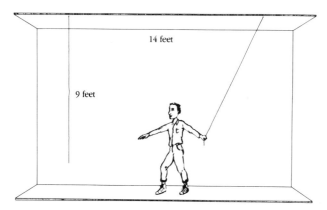

Figure 4.1: The Two-String Test. How can you tie the two strings together? You may use either a rattrap or a spring-type clothspin as an aid. Neither of these is long enough so that it could be used to reach the other string.

freedom, the ability to see new and unusual functions for familiar objects.

A graduate student in psychology studied the two-string problem and said, "I've got it! The answer is the rattrap. You catch a bunch of rats until you get one that isn't seriously hurt. You make a pet of it, then train it to be a 'trapeze' rat. It'll grab on to one of the strings and swing until it is able to get over to you while you're holding the other string!"

This is certainly an imaginative solution. Nonetheless, it is still a good example of functional fixity. It is predicated on the idea that a rattrap can be used only to capture rats. The solution might work, but how much more complicated it is than simply using the trap as a weight!

One young nun who tried to solve the problem decided that the rattrap and clothspin were being used us ruses. "You're just trying to confuse me," she said. "I know what I can use." Lifting the apron of her habit, she seized the oversized rosary beads hanging from her belt, and whirled them around her head while holding one of the strings. The beads caught onto the other string and she was able to get hold of it. Beaming with satisfaction, she tied the strings together while those watching applauded. Although her inability to consider other uses for the clothespin and rattrap shows functional fixity, her novel use of the rosary beads demonstrates functional freedom. Thus, functional freedom isn't an all-or-nothing construct; for example, someone may be functionally free when it comes to social thinking (i.e., working out a problem with a friend), yet functionally fixed in the face of a mechanical problem (how to open a stuck-shut window).

The Two-String Test is a simple illustration of how rigidity can creep into thinking patterns. The effects of schooling on functional freedom are shocking. A number of studies (e.g., Dacey and Ripple, 1967) have used the Two-String Test to measure students' functional freedom. Researchers found that about 90 percent of sixth graders were able to reach the "weighted string" solution within the fifteen minutes allowed (we've never heard of any other solution that uses only the materials given). Of ninth graders, 80 percent could do so, yet only 50 percent of college students were successful. Incredibly, a mere 20 percent of graduate students achieved a solution.

What's the conclusion? One view is that traditional schooling interferes with functional freedom. In addition, education encourages complexity of thought, which is likely to support a convoluted problem-solving style. (Remember our rat-training graduate student?) This works against producing simple ideas, which comprise many of the world's greatest solutions. Fortunately, there are many things parents can do to prevent education from destroying their children's functional freedom. In Chapter 14, "The Nurturing School," we describe them in detail.

Functionally free kids are easy to recognize. They are the ones who pipe up with the simple solution that went over everyone's head. They love to rearrange their rooms, to build things out of whatever's handy, to take toys apart and invent new uses for them. These children are terrific in emergencies where the ability to improvise can be so vital. They often enjoy nature and camping—where vines, sticks, rocks, and trees are all fodder to fertile imaginations.

While functional freedom points the way to fresh beginnings, functional fixity can lead to dead ends in family dynamics. When parents and children become functionally fixed, they lock themselves into positions of "Because I said so" authority and "You can't make me" defiance. Problem-solving becomes impossible. If harmony is to be restored, family members must step out of old mind-sets and brainstorm new approaches. Even the most difficult conflicts can be resolved once parents and children are able to abandon preconceptions and search for solutions that respect everyone's needs and feelings. The kids in our study are able to do this. They possess a trait called "stimulus freedom," which operates hand in hand with functional freedom (in Chapter 5 you will see how to recognize and foster this important cognitive trait).

ACTIVITIES TO FOSTER THE TRAIT OF FUNCTIONAL FREEDOM

CRITTER TRAINING

Materials: one live critter (a worm, cricket, grasshopper, beetle, ant, or similar); one critter habitat (pan or cardboard box with soil); a bell, hairdryer, other objects to be selected by child.

Tell your child to gently place the little critter in its new temporary habitat. Most of us think of these insects as pests. However, each of them has the ability to learn simple tricks. For example, place a worm on the surface of a bowl of dirt. Ring the bell; then with the use of a hairdryer set on low, blow warm air on the worm. You will find that the worm quickly attempts to dig its way into the soil. After several repetitions of this, just ringing the bell will make the worm dive for cover. Ask your child why he thinks this happens?

If you would like to try some variations on this theme, have your child train a variety of critters to learn new behaviors. For example, cover half of the bottom of a deep cake dish with white paper. Place a few ants on the white paper. Now gently blow warm air from the hairdryer (or ring a loud bell, or flash a bright light) over the ants on the white side. They will scurry to the other side of the pan. Repeat this procedure several times, and soon you will see the ants run from the white paper as soon as they are placed on it—without waiting for the stimulus.

Seeing how well these little critters can learn will change your child's view of them as well as encourage her functional freedom. Who says you can't teach an old worm new tricks?

HOW MANY USES?

On the road and the children are restless? Ask them:
"How many uses can you think of for:

a candle?
socks with holes in them?
a sponge?
a hammer?
peanut butter?"

Wild answers are great. Here are some examples for peanut butter: As sunscreen lotion. Or caulking around leaky windows. How about for hair mousse? Nose or ear plugs? (Yicch.) Stuntmen could fill a swimming pool full of peanut butter to use as a cushion when they fall off of buildings.

After the kids have gotten the hang of this game with funny or silly ideas, suggest that they take on more serious problems. For example, what are all the valuable uses to the community they can think of for:

garbage	old tires
newspapers	worn-out clothes
toxic fumes	teenagers who have dropped out of school.

HOW AM I SUPPOSED TO PAINT WITHOUT A PAINTBRUSH!

Materials: paint and assorted alternate painting implements.

Challenge your child to paint without using conventional brushes or fingers. Ask her what else she could use; examples of unique paint "brushes" include feathers, paper strips, pencils, leaves, Q-tips, sponges, cooked spaghetti, etcetera. With young children, you may have to veto certain suggestions due to the value of the object (Daddy's watchband, the fringes on Mommy's shawl), but be sure to acknowledge that they indeed could be used, if it weren't for the fact that they may not be!

Once your child has gathered her objects together, ask her to predict what each stroke will look like before she actually begins to paint. This consideration of cause and effect helps her to be more flexible in the way she thinks about things. Learning to predict consequences in order to shape behavior is one of the most valuable skills a child can have. When real-life problems confront your child, encourage her to look at the options she faces as "objects" with which to "brush" a solution; her task is to anticipate the effect of each, and to choose the most appropriate one.

This game also works well with small groups of children. Suggest to your child that he challenge his friends with this problem. Follow them as they go about the house looking for "paintbrushes." One of the best ways to promote functional freedom is to question children when they reject an object you think might be used as a brush. Ask them, "Are you sure that [knife, leaf, spoon, and so on] can't be used?" If they are blocked at first in coming up with ideas, you may want to demonstrate a technique yourself. For example, show them what an interesting paintbrush an elbow makes!

THE PLANTS ARE DYEING!

Materials: stove; large pots; large bowls; white cotton material such as old towels, T-shirts, or handkerchiefs; a variety of plants and vegetables.

Who would think to boil plants and vegetables in order to obtain different colored dyes? Functionally free forebears, that's who! Engage your child in a discussion about all the possible uses of plants, and see if you can't guide her to come up with the idea of boiling various plants and vegetables to produce dyes. Then, gather a selection for your experiment. Some (like beets and certain squashes) will work well; others won't. Let your child discover this for herself. Have her try to predict the color each plant will produce when boiled. Once the water becomes colored, let it cool, and then soak the fabric in it. See if the color transfers to the material.

Ask your child if she can think of any uses for the newly dyed fabrics. Perhaps they could be tailored into camouflaged uniforms and tents for toy soldiers, or put into service as patches for blue jeans. Anytime a child finds a way to turn castoffs or throwaways into useful items, functional freedom has been cultivated.

REINVENTING THE WHEEL

Materials: pencil and paper.

This activity fosters functional freedom not only by encouraging children to consider how objects function, but by getting them to think up functions for which no objects yet exist!

Pick an object that is interesting or important to your child and his friends—a bike, a pair of running shoes, a stereo. Tell them that you would like their help in inventing a new and improved version. Have them think of the various attributes and functions of the item, and then think of ways these could be improved. For example, a pair of Walkman headphones that could double as earmuffs in winter, a heated face mask for cold-weather sports, a glow-in-the-dark bicycle for better safety, a piggy bank with a timer that would dole allowances out to spendthrift kids at a slow and steady rate, etcetera. As the kids become more adept at this, they can bypass using existing objects as catalysts and instead think in terms of pure function: a device that would allow children to check for monsters under the bed without leaving the safety of their covers, a way to read a book while lying on one's back without having to hold it up.

Have the children draw or make models of their inventions. If they think they've come up with a winner, encourage them to look into the process of obtaining a patent and developing the invention.

OTHER ACTIVITIES

• Could you use a "versatile vacuum"? A "flexible fridge"? A "helpful hairdryer"? An "inventive iron"? Suggest to your child that he try to imagine alternative uses for your home appliances. For example, an iron might be used to take the wrinkles out of an inadvertently crumpled paper, or to warm up mittens before going out on a frigid day. An old refrigerator might be used to store a prized collection of books (keeps the dust and pollutants off them) or to maintain the freshness of unused rolls of film. The vacuum cleaner might be used to give the family dog a treat by reversing the hose connection and blowing it in her face (ever notice how dogs love to stick their heads out of open car windows?). A hairdryer might be employed to dry off a computer disk that has had water spilled on it.

• "Daddy, what makes the thunder?" Of course you might reply, "Well, under certain atmospheric conditions, blah, blah, blah . . ." Or you might try to get your child to dream up her own reasons for weather conditions. For example, perhaps a giant with a bad cough is making the thunder. Maybe the waves exist to wash off the dirty beaches. It could be that the wind is looking for a chance to make electricity; all that's needed is for us to build a windmill.

• "Please set the table for dinner, dear, and, uh, don't use any of the usual things!" What a challenge! What could be used instead of plates and glasses, knives and forks? Lids of bottles, jam jars, sharp sticks, screwdrivers, etcetera.

• Throughout this book, we will be giving examples of how to model behaviors you want your child to follow. If you try, you will be able to demonstrate functional freedom in the child's presence many times during the week. Want to roll out some pie dough? Don't grab the rolling pin—use a coffee can or a wine bottle. Need a weight? Don't reach for an ashtray—throw some pennies in an old sock. When he sees you being functionally flexible, he will pick it up almost by osmosis!

• "It's not only a great dessert topping, but it will remove almost any stain!" Have you seen this advertisement? Neither have we, but if you did, it would catch your interest, wouldn't it? Show your child some magazine advertisements, and ask him to think of how the ad could be rewritten, praising the product for some entirely different use.

• Pick out a few common household tasks, and help your child brainstorm some alternative means of completing them. For example, bathing the family pet can be a pain—nobody wants to do it. Perhaps you could rig up a mini-carwash in the back yard. Just park the dog inside, turn on the faucet, and presto! A completely clean critter.

While we're on the bathing scene, what about bath towels? Aren't those soggy old things often left lying around your house? What if we were able to jump out of the shower, and then step into the "drying area," a new part of the bathroom that blows us thoroughly dry in moments. Well, maybe that's not too practical, but you get the idea. Who knows? Your child will not only get practice in functionally free thinking, but you just might get a couple of really useful ideas.

• Organize a "functional freedom" scavenger hunt. Ask your child and several friends to find five things that could each serve the same purpose. For instance, what are five things that could be used as a plant holder? A musical instrument? A writing implement? A time keeper? A hat for the cat?

THE TWO-STRING TEST

Set up the Two-String Test (pages 52–53) in your house or backyard. Have your kids and the neighborhood kids try it. (Might as well encourage everyone's functional freedom!)

5

THE "AHA" EXPERIENCE: STIMULUS FREEDOM

THE STORY-WRITING TEST

Make up a story about the picture below. Be as descriptive and imaginative as you can. Think of a story no one else would. Take up to eight minutes to complete it.

Figure 5.1: The Story-Writing Test

In one study of creativity (Dacey and Ripple, 1967), 1,200 junior and senior high school students from three different states took this test. Amazingly, about nine hundred of the stories were almost exactly alike! They went something like this:

Once upon a time there was a cat named Tom. He was very curious. One day he was looking around and spied a suspicious-looking box. He heard a scratching noise coming from it. He lifted up one side and there he saw a mouse named Jerry. Jerry was a fat little mouse, and looked delicious. Without thinking, he made a grab for Jerry. The box crashed down on him and broke his head (skull, neck, back, etcetera)! That was how curiosity killed the cat!

Yawn. Not very imaginative. The other three hundred stories, however, were infinitely more variable, as this example written by an eighth grader shows:

Joe, the chipmunk, was chasing a butterfly. He was starving.

The sky overhead was streaked with clouds, the sun when it showed barely filtered through the trees, the burnt floor of the forest made the day seem completely gloomy. Joe wondered how he was going to get any food. He thought of last night—the men, the monsters. Some had four sharp claws, others had huge round eyes and pointed teeth. Joe was so scared!

Suddenly a bear jumped out of the bushes and was after him. He ran to a stream and started swimming. He was safe—only for a little, but . . . [The story stops here because time ran out.]

What is the major difference between the two groups of stories? The children who wrote the common stories were constrained by the lines that surround the picture. In effect, they penned their imagination within a fence of self-imposed rules:

"It is forbidden to tell a story that 'leaves' the square boundaries of the picture."

"A small animal with whiskers must be a cat."

"All cats should be named Tom (and all mice—Jerry)."

"Curiosity always kills the cat."

If you were to reread the instructions for this exercise, you would see that they do not include any prohibitions at all—in fact, they explicitly encourage farfetched imagination. Nevertheless, the first group of writers assumed a host of implicit limitations, and under those circumstances, it isn't surprising that there wasn't much to write about.

The children who wrote the more creative stories frequently

used the small square in the picture merely as a departure point from which they could travel to other, more exotic lands. Many saw it as a window or a door through which they could exit the picture's frame. Others stretched their imaginations to describe it as a house made of fish, a time capsule, a player piano. A small number (as in the story above) disregarded the square altogether.

The trait illustrated by this activity is a form of mental flexibility known as *stimulus freedom*. It has two aspects. First, when the stated rules of a situation interfere with the creative ideas of people who have stimulus freedom, they are likely to bend the rules to their needs. Second, and more important, they do not assume that rules exist when the situation is ambiguous.

Stimulus freedom and functional freedom differ in that functional freedom applies to attitudes toward *the use of objects,* whereas stimulus freedom applies to attitudes toward *the rules governing situations.* While the distinction may seem a minor one, each of these traits played a distinct role in the personalities of the children we studied.

Ability to solve the Nine-Dot Problem provides another good example of stimulus freedom.

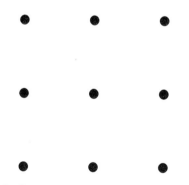

Figure 5.2: The Nine-Dot Problem. Can you connect
these dots with four straight lines, without taking your pencil
off the paper?

Frustrated? Here's a clue. Most people assume that the nine dots described a square, and that the solution lies *within* that square. (Just like most kids assume that their story has to lie within the square of the picture.) Thus they will fail to solve the puzzle.

The solution can be found only by leaving the square: by extending lines *beyond* the imagined boundary formed by the dots. This involves the ability to break free from self-imposed assumptions, to look beyond the obvious. Now try the puzzle again. Breakthrough? For many, it comes quite easily at this point. And if it does, you can see that you were blocked, not by stupidity, but by a needlessly narrow point of view.

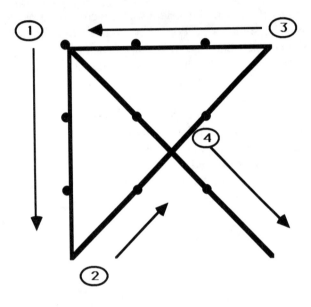

Figure 5.3: Solution to Nine-Dot Problem

"Stimulus-bound" children are swaddled in self-limiting doubts:

"I can't."
"I don't know how."
"It's too hard."
"I'll watch."
"You go first."
"Can't you do it for me?"

While this diverts the responsibility for failure ("I only did what she did...."), it also precludes the satisfaction of success. Fear of failure is one of the most effective inhibitors of personality growth.

Children who have stimulus freedom would rather err on the side of action. Their play varies; a favorite game or make-believe can have endless incarnations as roles and rules are reinvented. It doesn't matter if "it's not supposed to be like that." Rules are at their service, not the other way around.

Stimulus freedom is a trait that all children possess from a very young age. The following examples show stimulus freedom at work:

The toddler tries unsuccessfully to cram a square block into a round hole. At the edge of frustration, she suddenly discards the square in favor of the circle. With a gleeful shout, she triumphantly slips the round block into the hole.

The little boy struggles on tiptoe to climb into a big easy chair. Despite his valiant efforts, he is still too small to pull himself up. Pausing forlornly, he looks about the room. Seconds later, he drags a footstool across the carpet and places it in front of the chair. Having now divided the climb in two, he scampers up to savor his lofty success.

The 6-year-old wants to wheel his bike out of the garage. But Daddy parked crooked, and the gap between the car and the garage-door frame is too narrow for the bike's wide handlebars. He pushes mightily but to no avail. Finally, he lifts the front wheel off the ground so that the handlebars pass *above* the trunk of the car. The bike now rolls effortlessly out of the garage, and our young cyclist will soon feel the wind upon his face.

Meredith is madly in love with Michael, the new, shy boy in math. "He is sooo cute," she swoons to her best friend. "But he doesn't even know I exist. I've sent him notes, and called him, and I even told Laura to tell Kristen to tell Andy to tell Michael that I like him." Meredith groans. "Nothing works." After thinking it over, she decides that if nothing works, maybe she should do nothing—just play it cool for a while. Three days later, Michael asks her if she wants to go see the horror movie with him.

All parents have witnessed these magical moments, when they can almost see the gears turn inside their child's head. Such occasions can be fostered:

• Look for even the smallest signs of your child exercising stimulus freedom. Comment on them and praise them. (Yes, this is the "good" kind of praise!)

"Look at you! You thought up a whole new way of doing that!"

"You're right. There's no rule that says you have to do it the way everyone else does."

• Help your child recognize moments of cognitive breakthrough by introducing stimulus freedom as a strategy he can count on.

"Did you notice how the problem disappeared as soon as you thought about it in a new way?"

"Let's throw out all the rules and everything everyone says you're supposed to do."

"Maybe we can unstick our thinking . . ."

• Turn the "Aha!" experience into a family tradition. If you see stimulus freedom guiding your child around an obstacle, recognize the moment with an "Aha!" Ask your child to tell you what led to her success or progress. Often she'll reply with evidence of stimulus freedom: "I realized I didn't have to _____ "; "Nobody said you couldn't _____ "; "I changed the way I was trying to think about it."

Sometimes, though, an excess of stimulus freedom can lead children astray, particularly when combined with an affinity for risk-taking (see Chapter 12: "Tolerance of Ambiguity"):

> *While playing in the woods, the kids came upon a fence strung with "No Trespassing" signs. They skid to a halt. "What're ya doin'?" Peter asks as Tracy climbs over the fence. "It says no trespassing."*
>
> *"That's just if you're gonna do something wrong," Tracy replies. "Like cut down a tree or start a fire or stuff like that. It doesn't mean we can't go in there. We're just playing."*

Common sense and a concern for safety will tell parents when their children's rule-bending might be dangerous or unwise. Children have to know they're their *not* free to make up their own rules if it would put them or others in danger, or trespass upon the rights of others.

A child's innate stimulus freedom must be protected, for as the child matures, he will come in contact with many forces seeking its destruction. The two greatest enemies of stimulus freedom are:

- the fear of failure
- the belief that there is only one "right" way

CONQUERING THE FEAR OF FAILURE

Failure is an integral part of *healthy development*. No child would ever learn to walk if he were rescued, admonished, or plunked back in his playpen every time he toppled over when trying to stand up. Children have a natural drive to try and try again. Yet sooner or later, most children develop a fear of being wrong. They *learn* to respond to failure with shame, self-recrimination, or passivity. This fear can cripple a child's self-confidence. Fortunately, since it is a man-made fear, it can be corrected—and prevented:

- Teach by example. Show that it is all right to be wrong. Acknowledge to your child when *you* are wrong, and demonstrate your healthy attitude. "Oops, Mommy made a mistake."
- Glorify well-intentioned failure. Show your child that failure is his friend and teacher. Failure is a sign of effort, courage, progress, determination. It is a companion to success. Great inventions, explorations, and scientific discoveries would never have been achieved without an embrace of failure. Make sure he knows that.

"That didn't work, but what does it tell you?"

"Just think. Every failure means you're that much closer to success!"

- Help your child learn to laugh at her mistakes, and yours. Most mistakes can be corrected, undone, easily forgotten, or sufficiently apologized for. Why take them so seriously? Instead, show your child how to mitigate the consequences and move beyond them. In your efforts to cajole your child out of her misery, it's important not to belittle her feelings, though. Acknowledge that failure *can* feel bad. It *is* disappointing to uncover an error, to zoom into a deadend, or to realize that one must start all over again. However, even young children can be encouraged to look at failure with humor and philosophical acceptance if their parents model these attitudes themselves. Share examples from your own lives: it took eight attempts to quit smoking before you finally stopped; for every sale there are twenty rejections; you invited everyone at the office for dinner at your home and forgot to turn the oven on (carry-out Chinese food saved the day!).

THE BELIEF THAT THERE IS ONLY ONE RIGHT WAY

One study of a wide variety of classrooms found that approximately 90 percent of the questions asked by most teachers have only one right answer. When learning is presented solely in terms of right and wrong, what motivation does a child have to explore ideas and take intellectual chances?

From our own schooldays, we know that it's possible to get an A without having learned very much of importance: breathe in; retain-the-material-long-enough-to-take-the-test; breathe out.

Many of the "right answers" that kids learn in school are quickly forgotten. The resulting attitudes that children learn, however, are not so easily forgotten. These attitudes discourage children from questioning assumptions, from breaking the mold, from going beyond what's right to what's important. These attitudes, which in essence glorify The Right Way, squash stimulus freedom.

Granted, there are definitely right and wrong ways to accomplish certain tasks (such as defusing a bomb, for one), but isn't our definition of The Right Way often simply the way *we* learned to do something? How often are preference and tradition camouflaged as rightness?

Fortunately, there are many things parents can do to protect their child's stimulus freedom from the destructive effects of these rigid thinking patterns.

• Support your child against narrow definitions of rightness. Rightness is relative. What is the right way to get from New York to Los Angeles? It all depends—on the weather, the purpose of the trip, the time available, the finances of the traveler. Help your child realize that one person's "right" is someone else's "wrong." One method for doing this is to discuss the day's news stories. They contain many examples of individuals, organizations, and governments trumpeting the "right" way. Ask your child to use this construct to look at the values which underlie opposing positions on major political and social debates. What assumptions does each side make about "right ways" to think and act? Have your child make the case for the side with which he *disagrees*. It can also be helpful to view many of the tough issues children face growing up—drugs, sex, peer pressure—through this filter of different people's interpretations of "rightness." Encourage your child to question these definitions and, when necessary, to find his own right ways:

"Is that how *you* feel about it?"

"I can see why that might work for Ben, but what do you think is best for *you?*"

• When your child must participate in a system that demands its own brand of rightness—be it an institution or a rigid personality in a position of authority—lend support to your child's questioning attitude. This will help her to adapt to the reality. There's nothing wrong with saying, "I don't know why Mr. Marshall says this is the right way to do it. I think your way is right, too. But since he's the teacher . . ."

"I know, I'd better do it his way."

EXPANDING MIND-SETS

• Ask questions. Encourage experimentation.

"What's another way that you could do that?"

"Maybe you could look at it from a different angle."

"What do you think might happen if . . . ?"

Sometimes you'll have to show your child the way. But first, try to answer questions and suggest directions for thinking that will lead him to make the leap himself.

• Point out examples of stimulus freedom. The next time you're

faced with a similar problem, an understanding of stimulus freedom will help you to realize that often you already possess the
solution; all you need to do is enlarge or alter your mental frame
in order to gain access to it. A conscious awareness of one's own
limits can also help children to move beyond them. Have your
child try the Nine-Dot Problem (Figure 5.2). If she is successful,
ask her to describe the thinking process she used. If she gets
stuck, help her to break out of the "square." This can be done by
pointing out that she has drawn all the lines so that they stop at the
edge of the square. "What if the lines don't have to stop there? See
what happens if you try some other ways." After she has solved the
problem, or after you have shown her how it's done, discuss the
concept of stimulus freedom. Help her to see how solutions to
real-life problems are often blocked by limits we unknowingly
place on our thinking. Encourage her to take a new look at any
problems she currently faces.

• If a child feels an overwhelming urge to conform to peer
pressure, this can be an indication of a stimulus-bound personality. Early adolescence is probably the time when this danger is
greatest. Of course, the opposite can also happen. Sometimes
peer support provides the strength a child needs to challenge the
status quo and to explore the far reaches of imagination. How can
parents tell which one is happening?

Be receptive to your child's inviting her friends over to your
house. Offer to drive and to host. Take advantage of situations in
which you can unobtrusively get to know the people with whom
she spends her time. Which friends are open to forays of imagination and healthy new experiences? Which are fearful or restric-
tive in their attitudes? You must be careful not to criticize your
child's friends or attempt to control her friendships. Your sensitivity, however, will tell you which of your child's friendships to
encourage.

"JUMP STARTS" TO STIMULUS FREEDOM

Sometimes, altering one's surroundings is a good way to reach
stimulus freedom. Whenever you take a long walk or go for a

drive in order to think, you are using the environment to gain a fresh perspective. Stimulus freedom can also be enhanced by the use of rituals or trigger mechanisms:

In order to produce a state of inspiration, Schiller kept rotten apples in his desk; Shelley and Rousseau remained bareheaded in the sunshine; Bossuet worked in a cold room with his head wrapped in furs; Milton, Descartes, Leibniz and Rossini lay stretched out; Tycho Brahe and Leibniz secluded themselves for very long periods; Thoreau built his hermitage, Proust worked in a cork-lined room, Carlyle in a noiseproof chamber, and Balzac wore a monkish garb; Grety and Schiller immersed their feet in ice-cold water; Guido Reni could paint, and de Musset could write poetry, only when dressed in magnificent style; Mozart, following exercise; Lamennais, in a room of shadowy darkness, and D'Annunzia, Farnol and Frost only at night. The aesthetician, Baumgarten, advised poets seeking inspiration to ride on horseback, to drink wine in moderation, and, provided they were chaste, to look at beautiful women (Levey, 1940).

• Learn to recognize and support your child's thinking and creating rituals: the music, postures, settings, or times of the day he uses to free the mind. Even if they seem odd to you, so long as he is meeting his responsibilities, why oppose them?

"Because homework should be done at a desk."

"Because you can't concentrate with the music blaring." That's the old Right Way to Do Things trap. For some, background music is a distraction; for others, it's a protective cocoon of concentration. Maybe *you* can't work with music playing, maybe *you* need to sit at a desk in order to think, but why should your creativity triggers necessarily be the right ones for your child?

• Other environmental aids that can help to trigger your child's creativity and self-discipline and broaden her mental landscape might include:

a thinking cap;

a redesigned work space (let her take the lead in its reconfiguration);

a particular outfit (problem-plagued schools have been amazed to discover the extent to which dress codes or uniforms can improve student behavior and achievement—but it is not very surprising once you consider that a dress code is really nothing more than a trigger for changing self-image);

a secret cubby for hiding out and daydreaming;

a walk around the block before settling down to work;

a friend—many children find it easier to think when they are in the company of others so engaged.

Share some of the rituals famous creators have used. Then encourage your child to come up with her own ideas for thinking tools and triggers.

When kids reject convention to find invention, they become endowed with confidence. Children with this trait are well prepared to solve the puzzles of real life. Instead of giving up, they will say, "Hmm, maybe I should try a different approach." Sometimes this means taking things slowly—being patient, waiting for additional information, getting help from someone older, looking for a better opportunity to try again. Not surprisingly, we found that the ability to delay gratification was essential to the success of the creative, capable children we studied. That is the subject of the next chapter.

ACTIVITIES TO FOSTER THE TRAIT OF STIMULUS FREEDOM

BLACK MAGIC

Participants: five children; three are "guinea pigs" for the game, the other two (the "outsider" and the "pointer") are in cahoots with each other to pull off the "black magic."

The game is perfect for group stimulus-freedom-raising! One child, the "outsider," leaves the room while at least four others (including the "pointer") pick an object which will be "it." When the outsider is called back in, he has to guess which object is "it." This is done by having the pointer point to things in the room until "it" is pointed to, at which time the outsider will say, "That's it." How does he do that? It's up to the other children to figure out.

Unknown to children who remain in the room, the pointer is in on the game from the beginning. By prearrangement, he and the outsider have agreed that the pointer will point to various objects until he reaches a black one; the object he points to *next* will always be the one designated as "it." The game continues in this fashion, with new objects as "its," and the same child going out of the room and the same child acting as pointer, until one of the other children figures out how it's done.

Children need stimulus freedom to figure out the secret of the game. They must break free from the obvious ideas: that the trick was achieved by peeking through the keyhole, or listening at the door. Even after deducing that the outsider and the pointer must be collaborators, kids must use stimulus freedom to catch the signal being used—maybe it's a look, a sound, a body position, a pattern of pointing, a secret word slipped into a sentence.

Once the key to the black magic has been discovered, the game need not stop. All that's needed for play to continue is a new pair of "kids in cahoots" to plot a different strategy by which one of them will communicate which object is "it" (the third object after the piano; the object after the pointer clears her throat, the object after the pointer scratches his nose, etcetera). Even though the kids playing will now know that there is a prearranged signal by which the pointer indicates which object is "it," they won't know what it is.

THE ALPHABET PEOPLE

Materials: paper, pencils, crayons, construction materials.

Give your child a four-inch version of his first initial, cut out of heavy paper. Supply a variety of drawing and construction materials such as colored paper, crayons, scissors, pieces of cloth, glitter, and glue. Ask your child to turn the letter into a person. He might draw features, cut out clothes, provide hair, or subsume the letter as an arm or leg in a much larger construction. When he has finished, he might try to turn a new letter or number into a person.

This game can have endless variations: letters can be transformed into animals; letters can be transformed into scenes and objects—a storefront, a sailboat, a soda machine.

This game can also be played as a drawing game where one person draws something, and the other person has to turn it into an object. The stimulus drawing must be rich enough in detail or shape to pose a challenge, without being so complex as to foreclose possibilities.

DREAM ON

Materials: paper, pencil.

Ask your child to describe a recent dream to you in as much detail as possible. Write down all the details that you can. Explain to your child that dreams can mean something other than what they seem. Tell her that dreams are like treasure hunts; they have lots of clues and it's up to you to decide what they mean.

Ask your child why she thinks she may have had a certain dream. Point out specific details and ask her what she thinks they mean; Why did the elevator stop at the *seventh* floor? How come the car was going backwards? Why wasn't there any water in the lake?

There are no right answers. The goal is to encourage your child to come up with as many different interpretations as she can. Sometimes, children will come upon startling explanations and powerful feelings, particularly when dreams involve people they know and/or love. When undertaking this activity, parents should be sure that there will be enough time to talk about any issues that arise.

If your child has difficulty remembering her dreams, give her a pad of paper and pencil to keep next to her bed. Suggest that she write down everything she can remember about her dreams as soon as she wakes up. (Children who can't yet write can dictate.)

Sometimes it's helpful to use the "robin and worm" technique. If she can't remember the details of a dream, tell her to let her mind go blank. Usually a little piece of the dream, some tiny detail, will peek into her consciousness. If she follows that glimpse, she will remember more and more, until soon enough, like a robin pulling a worm out of the ground, the full-blown dream will be revealed.

OTHER ACTIVITIES

• Present the Nine-Dot Problem to your child (pages 63–64).

• Suggest that your child bend over and look at the world upside down through her legs. It's amazing how things change once you look at them with a fresh perspective. Have her describe what she sees—be it a tree, mountain range, parking lot, or back-yard swing set. Encourage her to use her imagination: does upside-downness transform the objects or landscapes and make them look like something else? Do the colors or sounds she observes change? Older children could photograph a scene right side up, and then photograph the same view upside down through their legs. Do the pictures differ? If so, how? And why?

• Draw a simple, dull picture, like the one that opened this chapter: a set of footprints going across a floor and up a wall; a large sphere in the middle of a street; a banana lying on a table, and so on. It might involve a subject or activity your child is interested in such as bike riding, monsters, horses, etcetera. Show the picture to your child and ask him to tell you the wildest, craziest, most imaginative story he can about the picture. Ask older children to tell you a second story, completely different from the first one, but based on the same picture.

• Children are usually good at finding ways to turn stumbling blocks into stepping stones. Tell your child that you're going to present her with a list of problems, disappointments or tragedies. Her job is to think of something good that might result from each event: a power failure could lead to making s'mores with the whole family gathered around the fireplace; failing a test could lead to special tutoring and a new friendship with the teacher, and so on. Ask her what good things have come from bad events in her own life.

• After reading your child a favorite story, go back to the start of the story and tell her that you and she are going to tell the story in a new way. This could be from a cross-gender perspective (i.e., if Goldilocks were a boy instead of a girl), from the point of view of a less central character (i.e., one of the three bears or one of Santa's elves), from the point of view of an inanimate "character" (i.e., Hans Brinker's skates, *The Polar Express* train), or even from the perspective of a brand new character your child introduces into the plot.

Write down the new versions and use them as the basis for other "new" versions, until the story line moves further and further away from the original.

• Give your child a colored sheet of paper on which a number of geometric figures (squares, triangles, circles) are drawn. Ask him to cut out the figures and make something out of them. If he needs help in thinking about what to make, suggest that it could be something to hang by his bed, or to put on the window sill; it could be something by which to remember a friend or experience. It's best to try to avoid suggesting specific things such as a house, car, or bridge, which limit your child's imagination.

Extend the activity by drawing and cutting out just one new figure. Now have your child make his *own* shapes to add to it in order to produce something unusual.

6

WAITING FOR GOOD DOUGH:
DELAY OF GRATIFICATION

*R*emember when you were a child and your parents said to you, "You can't have dessert until you've finished your dinner!"? And you wondered what difference it made, since the food all ends up in the same place anyhow? Did you figure your parents were just hung up on oral matters, having never resolved their "edible complex"? Well, guess what? It wasn't just your nutrition they nurtured. It was also your ability to *delay gratification.*

This trait is characterized by the willingness to endure the stress of prolonged effort so as to reap higher rewards. It is vital to a healthy personality. It is also at odds with the nature of childhood. Think how many of a child's statements boil down to "I want what I want and I want it NOW!"

Many of a child's tantrums, and many of a parent's "No's" revolve around the thwarting of immediate gratification. If kids by their very nature are in a great hurry to seek, to sow, and to reap, it's the culture that eggs them on. We live in "the Instant Era." Add water, stir, and your dreams (or at least a lot of your dinners) materialize before your eyes. Buy now, pay later. Fax, Fed Ex, and phones in the car. *ASAP. I need it by yesterday.*

In TV land (which children inhabit for more hours than they do school), dreams come true on the half hour. Commercials promise immediate rewards as well—if we only choose the right shampoo or soft drink.

What message do kids get from a society as quick on the draw as ours? That reward comes with little effort. That relationships are built overnight. That something is wrong if you're 25 and aren't rich and happy yet.

How much teenage depression and suicide (now the number

two cause of teenage death!) result from an inability to withstand pressures for instant success? How much drug use comes from a desire to change feelings as quickly as channels? How much crime results from the media-fed belief that life owes satisfaction on demand?

Of course, this is not to argue for self-denial and five-year courtships. Technology *is* liberating. Efficiency *is* admirable. Creativity, too, is enhanced by the march—or shall we say, the hundred-yard-dash—of progress.

But in becoming a society that worships *product*, we have neglected to teach children the joy of *process*. While delaying gratification may sometimes feel like a trip through hell, it is ultimately about joy, about the process of working for, waiting for, and finally rejoicing in greater pleasure.

HELPING CHILDREN LEARN TO DELAY GRATIFICATION

To help children learn to delay gratification, first recognize that you're up against two powerful forces: evolution (survival demands the quick satisfaction of needs), and culture (opinion-makers reinforce it).

• Encourage your child to have goals that are within her capabilities. Unrealistic expectations for achievement will lead her to frustration and a sense of failure. These feelings will undermine her motivation to work toward distant goals. Where appropriate, suggest modest beginnings as a prelude to more grandiose ends. For example, movie stardom might begin with a role in the school play or with joining a children's theater; learning to skate backwards might be a good initial goal toward an Olympic gold medal in figure skating.

• Celebrate milestones along the way to break a long wait into increments. If a child is saving his allowance to buy something, or counting the days until a happy event, recognize the occasion of being a quarter or half way there. Make sure he feels proud of what he's accomplished up to any given point. For example, keep a "thermometer" chart of his savings toward a new bike. Plan special events for difficult points on the chart: the purchase of a bicycling magazine at the quarter mark, a visit to the bike store at the halfway point.

• The incremental approach works for other projects, too. Large and distant goals are overwhelming to children. How can they possibly clean their WHOLE room, eat their WHOLE dinner, read a WHOLE book, write a WHOLE term paper? How can they ever save enough money to buy a WHOLE drum set, a WHOLE ski outfit, a WHOLE stereo system? But what they can do is break any project into smaller components.

Include your children in the planning and preparation of family events. The grandest Thanksgiving dinner can be seen as the sum of many parts and operations: stuffing, turkey, cranberry sauce, potatoes; shopping, cooking, setting the table. Family vacations are also made up of many smaller components: determining a budget, saving the money, scheduling the time, choosing a destination, making travel arrangements, finding a place to stay, selecting activities and points of interest to visit. Ask questions that encourage them to look at large goals in terms of component steps:

"What are all the things you'd have to do in order to accomplish that?"

"What do you think a good first step would be?"

"What are all the parts the architect had to think of when he designed that building?"

"How many steps do you think go into the making of a movie?"

"If we wanted to add a garage and family room onto the house, what are all the things we'd have to do?"

• Acknowledge how difficult it can be to defer pleasure. "It must be hard to save your money for the ski trip while all your friends are spending theirs on movies and food." Your empathy won't cause her to abandon her efforts, it will bolster her.

• Support your child's work on long-term projects (being careful not to take on responsibility for the project yourself). Praise him for his patience and perseverance. At times of frustration, offer sympathy and share your own stories of setbacks and triumphs. Volunteer assistance, as long as it's under your child's direction. A willing "sous-chef" can do wonders toward bucking up your child's flagging motivation.

CAUTION...

Many children are skilled dilettantes who race from one enthusiasm to another. Today's excitement turns into tomorrow's tedium. This presents parents with a frustrating dilemma. Naturally, we want to encourage our children's interests. But what do we do when those interests gather dust in the attic? When the cost of squandered piano, trumpet, guitar, tennis, karate, judo, and ballet lessons approaches the mortgage on the house? How do we know whether we're supporting a child's healthy need to experiment or his inability to delay gratification? Are we encouraging a passionate search for the right expressive outlet, or merely wastefulness?

It's difficult to say. Creativity *is* wasteful. The creative process rips through ideas and materials. It roars into dead ends. The fact that the ability to delay gratification is a necessary trait suggests that the creative path is a long one, strewn with setbacks and miscalculations. The child who shows little ability to persevere may not yet have found a compelling occasion to do so. However, perseverance *is* required to enjoy a new skill, as in learning to ski or to play a musical instrument.

Responsibility also requires delay of gratification, and some children really need to learn that. There are children, however, who are overly responsible. These kids don't have much fun because they're always putting off pleasure. They need to "lighten up" and gratify themselves! Empathy, too, means sometimes putting another's needs before your own. While some children are too self-centered to delay gratification in favor of someone else's needs, others worry and sacrifice for friends and family excessively.

The following considerations may help you to discover an effective balance between aggressive experimentation and overresponsibility:

• If your child zips from interest to interest like a bumblebee on speed, it may be that the initial choices he makes are inappropriate. They may be influenced by peer interests or by a desire to please parents or other adults. They may demand motor skills and intellectual concentration far beyond the capabilities of a child his age. He may be extremely sensitive to frustration and need your extra encouragement to surmount early obstacles. Allow him to pursue his dreams, but guide him to select goals that are realistic. Ask nonjudgmental questions that will help him to better understand his motives. Reflect on previous experiences if you feel they relate to the issue at hand. (Try to avoid *I told you so* implications, however, or making your child feel that he has to carry the baggage of his past with him wherever he goes.)

"That sounds great, but I thought you *hated* team sports. Did something happen to change your mind?"

"Boy, that would be a lot of hard work! How would you fit it into your schedule?"

"What a neat idea. But I thought you wanted to keep more time free to do things with your friends?"

• If your child has had an ongoing problem with concentration and commitment, or seems to avoid gratification excessively, by all means consult a professional. Your child may be as confused and upset as you are by her inability to follow through. She may be laboring under an ever-increasing burden of shame and self-reproach. Learning disabilities, hyperactivity, and/or attention deficit disorders could be the source of the problem. Once diagnosed, they can be effectively treated, and your child may feel transformed.

• To gain insight into your child's relationship to this trait, ask yourself these questions: Does he abandon ship at the first moment of frustration? Does he flee commitment out of self-doubt and fear? Does he jettison interests with a sense of victory or surrender? Is he "running from" or "running toward"?

• If an older child asks you to underwrite a new long-term project, ask her for a show of commitment. Most children will recognize this as parent language for "paying half." A child's willingness to ante up (with time, money, chores, or possessions) is an excellent way to assess motivation. (Conversely, *your* willingness to support your children's goals is an excellent way to motivate them.)

Finally, a word should be said in praise of dilettantism. Childhood is a time of experimentation. The marvelous quest for self-knowledge is an experiment whose results may not be known for years, but the ability to retrench after disappointment and retain hopeful attitudes are signs of strength.

Parent-child conflicts about delayed gratification may occur in part because much of the gratification that gets delayed in the average household is the parents': they defer plans, purchases, and peace and quiet in the service of raising their children. This sacrifice can make parents especially sensitive to a child's frequent demands for immediate pleasure.

"Sometimes it makes me furious," a father in our study confided, "how quickly my child loses interest in things. Don't get me wrong; I'm pleased that he shows interest in the first place and I try to support that. But when I see, two weeks later, that he's finished with the chemistry set, or given up on the model, well . . ."

This father is not alone in his feeling. But he was helped by being able to recall his own childhood. "There was a time when I wore out identities faster than sneakers. I remember my abstract artist phase after seeing an exhibit at the Whitney. Then for about a year (actually that was one of my longer interests), I played drums in just about every rock band in Suffolk County. And for about three weeks I decided I was going to be a poet, so I dressed in black and wrote about death and doomsday. Then summer came and it got too hot to wear black."

Part of the conflict arises because adults and children have very different relationships to time. For adults, time rushes like water over Niagara Falls. It is natural that they want to see their children set goals and demonstrate the perseverance to achieve them. Children, however, feel they are immortal. In the freshness of their youth, a week seems forever. And a year?! Inconceivable. As 6-year-olds looking at a life-span of 75 years, time is infinite, beyond their grasp: they'll work on those larger projects—the ones that take years if not lifetimes to complete—later. The art of life lies in finding a balance between daily pleasures and those deferred, in discovering the point of symbiosis where each feeds the other.

Thus the ability to delay gratification is critical, not only to a child's developing creativity, responsibility, and empathy, but to her fulfillment as a human being. No personality trait, however, stands alone.

ACTIVITIES TO FOSTER THE ABILITY TO DELAY GRATIFICATION

WRITE TO THE SOURCE

Materials: stationery, pen, postage.

Children are naturally interested in how products and ideas come into existence. Who invented Oreos? How does the cream get into a doughnut? What's the difference between jam, jelly, and preserves? Encourage your child to pursue the avenues of her curiosity by writing to manufacturers. (Consumer product addresses or toll-free service numbers are usually found on packages.) You might ask her to come up with her own hypotheses, which she could then include in her letter. Although it may take six weeks or more to receive a response, most companies will answer thoughtful letters from consumers, young or old. The task of waiting is offset by the excitement of receiving a very official-looking reply.

Authors of school textbooks may also be approached with reader questions, comments, and criticisms. In addition, children can write to the authors of their favorite books, care of the publishing company. (Be sure they don't write to Mark Twain or Louisa May Alcott. The resulting wait could strain even the most highly developed ability to delay gratification!)

TIME IN THE BOTTLE

Materials: one cookie can or Thermos bottle, assorted items.

By the end of each day, a child's pockets are like a time capsule—full of little items that tell the tale of his day's adventures.

Talk to your child about the nature of time capsules and suggest that he create his own—using a cookie can or Thermos bottle—to be buried outdoors and opened one to three months later. (For older children, increase the length of time, perhaps each birthday.) Help him brainstorm for items he would like to include, or allow him to turn the activity into his secret. Be sure to settle in advance on the "unburying" date, and mark it on a calendar. Knowing that he will open the buried capsule on a specific holiday or during a different season can encourage your child to approach this activity with whimsy and creativity.

You might suggest to your child that he create and stow away a time capsule that would not be opened for years—perhaps not until his tenth or sixteenth birthday!!

LEAVING ONE STONE UNTURNED

Materials: one large rock or brick.

Take your child for a walk in the woods or in a park. Look for an old brick or a rock that is implanted in the soil. Carefully turn it over and explore with your child the insect life hiding underneath. When you're done exploring, place the rock back in its original spot.

Upon your return home, give your child a rock or brick to put in a spot of her own choosing. Secure it in the ground and tell your child that you and she will return to look at the top of it frequently. "But we will have to wait a *very* long time before we can turn it over if we want insects and plants to make it their home."

Check the outside of the rock as often as your child would like, but remind her that if you and she overturn the rock too soon, the insects will not yet have had a chance to build their homes. Ask her to imagine what it might be like under the rock for insects. When about a month has passed, it is time to overturn the stone.

(You may wish to build additional incentives into the waiting period: after one week you'll take a picture of the rock; after two weeks you'll read a story about Willy the Worm, etcetera.)

WAIT AND SEE(D)

Materials: variety of seeds, dishpan of soil, string, paper, and pencil.

Gather up to twenty different kinds of seeds. You will need two of each. Get as much variety in your collection as possible. Include both vegetable and flower seeds.

Help your child fill a plastic dishpan full of dirt at least three inches deep. Have him mark off the surface in two-inch squares with pieces of string. Now it's time to plant: put two matching seeds in each of the squares. Make a map so that he will remember what is planted where.

Your child should keep a log of how many days pass before the seeds germinate and small plants appear on the surface. Ask family members to guess when the first and last seeds will sprout.

Depending on the seeds planted, it can take up to three weeks to see results. Be sure he keeps the soil moist and in a sunny spot.

SHOE BOX COLLECTIONS

Materials: shoe box, heavy tape, assorted items.

Present your child with a shoe box and some very heavy tape. Ask her to tape the box, using as much tape as she needs, in such a way that will prohibit anyone from opening the box. When she is done, suggest that she use the box for her own collection. Make a small opening (about an inch and a half square) at the top of the box with a knife.

Help your child to think of things she might collect that would fit through the slot: acorns, bottle caps, shells, buttons, and so on. Have her collect items over time, with the understanding that she will not peek through the slot or open the box until it is too full to fit anything more inside.

When the time comes to open the box, the reward of seeing her huge collection and becoming reacquainted with long-forgotten treasures may make her want to start a new one right away. By altering the shape and size of the slot, you can reorient the nature of the objects she will collect.

Older children can be encouraged to start collections of their own choosing: old books, baseball cards, coins, bottles, and the like.

WAITING FOR GOOD DOUGH

Materials: kitchen, food, recipes.

Cooking is an excellent way to help children learn to delay gratification. Set them up to bake gooey, chewy chocolate chip cookies, or brownies or some other favorite food. The only catch is that they have to wait unit the baking is done, the dishes are washed, the kitchen is clean, and the treat is cooled down to taste the product. Well worth waiting for!

A PICNIC OF SOUND

Here's a sound idea: take your child to a country field or nearby park. Spread out a blanket and lie down. Explain that you need to be perfectly quiet. At first you will only hear the most obvious sounds—birds, crickets, a jet flying overhead. But the longer you wait, the more new sounds you will hear: a distant truck, the hooting of an owl, the wind, a sound of hammering, a pine cone falling, the rat-a-ta-tat of a woodpecker. Tell your child to hold up his hand every time he hears a new sound. If he likes, he can whisper what he thinks it is in your ear. He may wish to tape record his sounds so that the rest of the family can try to guess what they are.

7

KNOW YOUR ORANGE:
THE BALANCED BRAIN

*I*s your brain unbalanced? Does your head tilt a little to the left or right? If so, we're afraid we can't help—the kind of balance we'll be talking about in this chapter involves the relationship between the right and left hemispheres of the brain. We are going to discuss why such balance is important, and describe ways to help your child achieve a balance in these two hemispheres. The following exercises help to illustrate the concept of a balanced brain. Give them a try!

The Ingenuity Test*
Complete the following statements by selecting the most accurate answer. You'll need to fill in the missing letters.

1. In the process of writing a report, several hundred reference books were used. A list of authors and titles of books was to be included at the end of the report for bibliographic references. In order to speed up the alphabetizing process for this bibliography, it was decided that each reference would be listed on a small

    a) n _ _ s.
    b) t _ _ r.
    c) r _ _ d.
    d) c _ _ d.
    e) s _ _ e.

2. Bob Johnson, a draftsman, keeps a compass in his desk drawer, along with a lot of other equipment he needs frequently. Since he has more equipment than adequate room to store it, the desk

---

*Adapted from the test developed by Dr. John Flanagan.

drawer is cluttered. Therefore, he has often pricked a finger on the compass point when reaching for a pencil or something else. To keep this from ever happening again, he embeds the compass point in an

  a) a _ _ _ _ l.
  b) e _ _ _ _ r.
  c) i _ _ _ _ d.
  d) a _ _ _ _ t.
  e) e _ _ _ _ e.

3. It is possible to add vertical lines to the pages of a notebook or to rule paper quickly and easily by using a handmade stamp and a regular stamp pad. This solution makes it possible to vary the thickness of the lines by changing the tension of the material used. This special stamp is made from a block of wood, several thumb-tacks, and three or four narrow

  a) r _ _ _ _ r b _ _ _ s.
  b) h _ _ _ _ t n _ _ _ s.
  c) t _ _ _ _ k s _ _ _ s.
  d) l _ _ _ _ e h _ _ _ s.
  e) o _ _ _ _ d u _ _ _ s.

4. A contractor was asked to build a two-bedroom house so that maximum use could be made of wall and cupboard space and so that housework could be kept to a minimum. The contractor eliminated a great deal of extra work by building a double-duty linen closet. This was made accessible from both bedrooms by placing one set of linen drawers between the two rooms. For each drawer, each room had a separate set of

  a) t _ _ _ _ _ s.
  b) g _ _ _ _ _ s.
  c) p _ _ _ _ _ s.
  d) h _ _ _ _ _ s.
  e) r _ _ _ _ _ s.

5. On an aircraft instrument panel it is very important to know whether certain of the auxiliary electrical systems are working at

all times. To keep the pilots informed, a light was installed that lit up when one of the systems was out of order. This caused confusion when the light bulb burned out, since the pilot then could not tell when the system was out of order. It was decided to change the circuit so that the old interpretation of the signal light was now

a) c _ _ _ _ _ d.
b) o _ _ _ _ _ n.
c) f _ _ _ _ _ t.
d) r _ _ _ _ _ d.
e) t _ _ _ _ _ r.

ANSWERS:

1. d) card.
2. b) eraser.
3. a) rubber bands.
4. d) handles.
5. d) reversed.

Why is a balanced brain essential to the development of a responsible, empathetic, and creative personality? And what's the connection between the Ingenuity Test and a balanced brain? In order to answer these questions, we need to back up and explain a bit about how the brain works.

The cerebral cortex—that part of the brain in which thinking, sensation, and perception occur—is divided into two hemispheres. In most people, one side is dominant over the other. This is called "lateral dominance," and can be seen soon after a child is born, when its movements develop into a pattern of preference for one hand, eye, and foot over the other. Right-handers tend to be dominated by the left side of the brain; left-handers tend to be dominated by the right side of the brain. This was first learned when it was noticed that damage to one side of the brain usually impairs the functioning of the *opposite* side of the body.

While each hemisphere's functions overlap to some degree with those of the other, the left side is primarily concerned with language and accuracy. The right side is more involved in imagination and nonverbal functions (music, dance, intuition), which is why it is often referred to as the "creative" half of the brain.

Creativity, however, requires more than just imagination. It also requires accuracy, analysis, and objectivity. Thus, creativity is not so much the product of a "pumped up" right hemisphere as it is the product of how well the *two* hemispheres of the brain *relate* to each other. It is when the right and left sides of the brain work together, with accuracy and imagination alternately leading and deferring, that the highly creative and capable personality develops. The other two core characteristics of the children in our study—responsibility and empathy—also depend on good communication between the two hemispheres of the brain. Responsibility has both a concrete side (for example, punctuality, doing homework, feeding the dog) and an abstract side (for instance, democracy, ethics). Empathy not only means being able to intuit how a friend is feeling, but also being able to analyze the conflicts that may be causing those feelings.

The Ingenuity Test is a measure of one's ability to combine the seemingly opposite kinds of thinking done by the two hemispheres. It does so in two steps:

• In order to solve each problem, you must think imaginatively, casting about for possible solutions that could fit the problem and staying open to all the possibilities suggested by those solutions. This type of open-ended thinking, in which you seek to *expand options*, is known as *divergent* thinking, and it is associated with the right side of the brain.

• After you have produced one or more guesses, you must then think accurately, selecting the particular word or phrase that you believe will best fit the story or situation that is described. This *narrowing of possibilities*, from the many to the one, is known as *convergent* thinking, and it takes place in the left side of the brain. Success on the Ingenuity Test requires frequent switching between the two hemispheres of the brain as convergent and divergent thinking are carried out.

Figure 7.1 on page 91 depicts the mental process people go through as they take the Ingenuity Test.

So much emphasis has been placed on the roles of *each* hemi-

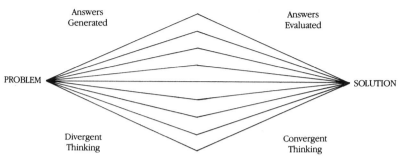

Figure 7.1: The Mental Process Used in Solving the *Ingenuity Test*

sphere that it has obscured the importance of the balance be-tween the two. While you can see from the list (on page 92) of dichotomies why the right side of the brain is often said to be the "creative" half, you can also see that without left hemisphere functions, creativity would be up the cognitive creek without a paddle.

The children in our study are adept at using both hemispheres in a balanced way, and achieve better communication between the two. In addition, they are adroit at knowing when to use each. Seemingly opposing functions are extraordinarily well-integrated.

Why is it so important to have a balanced brain? Let's take the example of a pediatrician. A successful pediatrician must maintain an active mental library of medical information; she must be able to think rationally and deductively, to approach patient complaints in a sequential way, to deal with finances, scheduling, supplies, and reports. These are all left-brain functions. At the same time, a pediatrician must be intuitive about her patients' needs and feel-ings and adept at reading facial expressions and body language. When searching for a diagnosis, she must follow hunches and think divergently, amassing a selection of possible diagnoses based on the symptoms present. To set her young patients at ease she must be warm and playful; to set their parents at ease, she must be empathetic. These are right-brain functions. You can see how the functions of each hemisphere illuminate and support those of the other.

If you go back and look at the list of right- and left-brain func-tions, and think of them in terms of the situations your child will

THE BRAIN'S CONTRASTING FUNCTIONS

Left Hemi-sphere		Right Hemi-sphere
Intellect	as opposed to	Intuition
Convergent	as opposed to	Divergent
Intellectual	as opposed to	Sensuous, emotional
Deductive	as opposed to	Imaginative
Rational	as opposed to	Metaphoric
Horizontal	as opposed to	Vertical
Discrete	as opposed to	Continuous
Concrete	as opposed to	Abstract
Realistic	as opposed to	Impulsive
Directed	as opposed to	Free
Differential	as opposed to	Existential
Sequential	as opposed to	Multiple
Historical	as opposed to	Timeless
Analytical	as opposed to	Synthetic, holistic
Explicit	as opposed to	Implicit
Objective	as opposed to	Subjective
Successive	as opposed to	Simultaneous

face in life—school, job, personal and professional relationships—you can see why the child who develops a balanced brain has distinct advantages over the child who does not.

This interhemispheric brain communication can be fostered by parents in a number of ways. One of them is to stimulate micro-neuron development. At the moment of conception, children inherit their *macro*neuronal system. Macroneurons form the main electrical pathways of the brain and appear to be the major vehicles for thought. *Micro*neurons, however—the tiny connectors that run between macroneuronal lines—continue to grow for the first year and a half. Research suggests that the stimulation of microneuronal development during the first year and a half of life can enhance a child's creative and intellectual development by increasing the number of possible pathways between macroneurons. It is likely that connections between the right and left hemispheres of the brain are also increased, because of microneurons in the corpus callosum (the band of fibers uniting the hemispheres). This can be done by providing the child with a moderately stimulating environment. Too much stimulation can be just as detrimental as too little! This is because stimulation must be *distinctive and meaningful* to promote cognitive growth. Research indicates that children raised in large families show poorer verbal development than those raised in smaller ones. Yet children in large families are likely to have more "stimulation"— noise, music, doors slamming, people coming and going, and so on. The difference lies in the *quality* of stimulation. While children raised in smaller families have less overall stimulation, the stimulation they do have tends to be more interactive, personalized, and meaningful. They also are more likely to be participants, rather than spectators, in the stimulation they receive. From the child's perspective, it may be the difference between being placed in a room where one's older siblings are playing, and being played with directly. At the opposite end of the spectrum, studies show that children suffer cognitive and social deficits from too little stimulation—not having enough opportunities for touching, playing, watching, and vocalizing.

While none of the parents in our study was explicitly aware of the importance of stimulating microneuronal growth during infancy, most of them had done so intuitively. They sang to their infants. They played soft and melodic music in the nursery. They created gentle environments with pastel colors and soothing talk. They provided the mild stimulation of little toy birds and mobiles above their babies' cribs. They provided enough sound and sensation to keep their children alert and engaged, but not so much as to irritate them.

We are often asked whether left-handed people are more creative than right-handed people. It does seem logical that if highly creative people are right-brain dominated, they would tend to be left-handed in greater numbers than the general population—and many famous creative people were: Leonardo da Vinci, Benjamin Franklin, Michelangelo, to name a few. But do the facts support this as a general thesis?

Scientists today identify two major causes of left-handedness: genetic inheritance and minimal brain damage to the left hemisphere, possibly during the birth process. Because of this damage, the person comes to rely more heavily than usual on the right side of the brain for language as well as for other functions.

Twins appear to be a special case of this. Although only about 8 percent of the population is left-handed (this figure used to be 5 percent, which was no doubt due to the practice in many schools of discouraging left-handed writing), twins are left-handed 25 percent of the time! This is true for both monozygotic (identical, single-egg) and dizygotic (fraternal, two-egg) twins. This could be explained by the minimal brain damage theory; some mothers of twins have smaller-than-average pelvises, so twins are squeezed together. It may also be that they bump heads and thus are more likely to suffer slight brain lesions.

Our research offers some support for the theory that creative people are disproportionately left-handed. Of those who scored in the lower half of the creativity scale in our study, 8 percent were left-handed. Of those who scored high in creativity, 20 percent were left-handed!

Historically, there has been a bias against left-handers. The French word for left is *gauche*, which means clumsy; the Latin word is *sinister*. The *American Heritage Dictionary* includes among its definitions of left-handed: "awkward, maladroit [against the right], obliquely derisive, dubious, and insincere, as in left-handed flattery." There are many allusions in the Bible that show a bias against the left. In earlier days, the left hands of left-handed children were sometimes bound to force them to use their right hands; most school desks and consumer products are designed with right-handed people in mind. While subtle biases against the left-handed may remain even today, they are a small disadvantage when considered in light of the increased right brain–left brain communication left-handers enjoy. Thus our advice to the parents of right handers is to encourage ambidextrousness.

During your child's first two years, place silverware, toys, and other objects in a "neutral" zone that favors neither her right nor her left hand. This way she is free to choose which to use. When you give her things directly, alternate putting them in her right and left hands, or offer them to her midway between her right and left sides and let her choose. Lateral dominance is strongly influenced by heredity, however, so do allow time for your child to become adept with her natural handedness.

After the age of two, your child's handedness should be apparent, and practice with the less-preferred hand can begin. Suggest that your child try the opposite than usual hand to do a task. This is not to say that you should try to *change* your child's preferred hand. Rather, challenge your child to practice writing, eating, ball-throwing, or teeth-brushing with the less-used hand. This exercise encourages a balanced brain by cultivating pathways through the corpus callosum, the bundle of nerves that connects the two hemispheres. The more of these pathways there are, the more inter-hemispheric communication is likely to occur.

ACTIVITIES TO FOSTER A BALANCED BRAIN

KNOW YOUR ORANGE

Materials: one orange for each child or adult (five participants is ideal); one large paper bag.

This activity fosters balanced brain use by forcing people to analyze a problem and plan a problem-solving strategy (left-brain functions), while using their sense of touch (a right-brain function).

Give each child an orange and tell him or her to "get to know it." Have the children study their oranges for size, bumps, dents, and any other noticeable traits. Then write the participants' names on the oranges with a felt-tipped pen, and place the oranges in a large bag. The children reach in one at a time without being allowed to look, and each child tries to find his orange. Amazingly, most of the time they can. Each child's orange is returned to the bag after his turn.

Next, ask the children to tell how they recognized their orange. Then ask them to suggest other objects that could be used for the game, and what identifying characteristics they would look for. Finally, see how many attributes they can think of to identify and/or define an object, such as its height, weight, smell, taste, use, meaning, historical origin, "bounceability," "squashability," and so on.

GIVE YOURSELF A HAND

Materials: pen or pencil, paper.

Tell your child (or a group of children) that in this activity they are going to learn to draw without looking at the paper while drawing. Get them going with these instructions:

Take your pen or pencil in your regular drawing hand and use its point to pierce through the center of a square of paper. The paper will act as a shield so you can't look at the drawing surface.

Place your other hand in an interesting but comfortable position in front of you. Focus your eyes on an edge of that hand and put the point of the pencil on the paper, making sure you are allowing enough room for drawing the entire hand. Be sure you can't see your drawing. Now pretend that you are a tiny ant traveling slowly along the edge of the hand you are going to draw, going in and out of every wrinkle and crevice. When you feel that you *are* that ant, and that the tip of your pencil is the nose of that ant, *slowly* move your eyes along the edge of your hand. As your eyes move—as the ant wanders through canyons and over hills, brushing past hairs and climbing over scars—move your pencil on the paper at the same slow pace. Match the movement of the pencil exactly with the movement of your eye (and your ant). Do not pause in the drawing and do not look at it. Continue at an even pace. Trust yourself. Trust your ant.

Extensions:

Reverse the procedure so that right-handed children draw with their *left* hand while holding their *right* hand in front of them. (Vice versa for left-handers.) This also gives practice in interhemispheric brain communication.

Encourage your child to choose other objects to draw "blind": toys, cups, plants, furniture. This activity also can be done outdoors. Trees, mountains, cloudscapes, and horizons all have clear edges that lend themselves well to this type of drawing.

As children become adept at this activity, let them try to sketch not only the outline, but details *within* the edges as well. This, of course, is much harder because it involves lifting the pencil from one spot on the paper to another without peeking.

ORIENTEERING

Materials: All you really need is an orienteering compass and map, but binoculars, a clipboard for holding maps, and basic hiking gear (sturdy shoes, canteen, etcetera) will increase your comfort and competence.

Most kids love to follow a treasure map to find a hidden treasure. The sport of orienteering is a structured sort of treasure hunt which involves using a map and a compass to navigate an outdoor course, usually in a wooded area, laid out by organizers of the event. Visual markers are attached to objects such as boulders, fence posts, or unusually shaped tree limbs. These "stations" are then marked on a map of the area. The goal is to move from station to station in the denoted order so that you arrive back at where you started in the shortest amount of time. The child, working with you, must combine visual, mathematical, and spatial abilities in order to follow the course. Orienteering not only exercises the interrelated use of several areas of the brain, but it's an excellent way to enjoy a few hours outdoors with your child. Participants range from novices to experts who race around the course competing for prizes, from families with small children to elderly persons out for a challenging stroll.

There are many local clubs that sponsor this activity. Look under "orienteering" in the Yellow Pages of your phone book. Two helpful books on the subject are: *Orienteering* by Hans Bengstton and George Atkinson (Brattleboro, Vermont: S. Greene

Press, 1977); and *Be Expert with Map and Compass* by Bjorn Kjellstrom (New York: Scribner's, 1976).

OTHER ACTIVITIES

• During the course of a meal, encourage your child to think about the taste of one of the foods being served. For example, while eating dessert, you might say, "What does this dessert make you think of?" "What music does this dessert remind you of?" "What television programs?" "What colors?" "What emotions does it make you feel?"

• Without your child seeing what you are doing, in four small bowls, place four substances that have very different textures (cold cooked macaroni, cornmeal, Jell-O, cornstarch mixed with water, wet doughnuts, rice). In four other bowls place four substances that have very different smells (damp earth, curry powder, goat cheese, watermelon, musty papers). Blindfold your child and present one smell to him. Have him describe the smell, what it reminds him of, what kinds of emotions it makes him feel. Now have him touch a different substance. Ask him the same kinds of questions. Do not let him know that what he is touching and what he is smelling are two different things. Now ask him to tell you what he thinks it is.

• Select a word from the dictionary that you think your child doesn't know. Try to pick a word that evokes visual images (i.e., strident, snit, lugubrious). Now provide her with a pencil or crayons and paper and ask her to draw a picture of what the word means. This activity is fun to conduct with several children together. The commerical game of *Pictionary* is a good model for this.

One variation of this game is to make players draw with the hand they are not accustomed to using. Another variation is to play some music that your child is unused to hearing, and have her draw pictures of the music. Making up stories about music is another good way to practice balanced use of the brain. Here, too, stories need not interpret the music literally; the music is there as a springboard to the imagination.

• Organize a scavenger hunt—except that the items to be found are sounds. Players will need tape recorders in order to keep a record of the sounds they find or create. The first time children play the game, the list of sounds they are told to find might be quite liberal, for example: clinking, dripping, swishing, squeaking, scraping. As children become more practiced, the list might include less well-defined concepts such as the sounds of green, red, happiness, freedom, laziness, quickness, thoughtfulness, emptiness, and fear. Children must switch between the abstract, metaphoric, and emotional right brain, and the concrete, logical left brain to do this activity.

• Make a family tradition out of combining two words to make a better one. For example: flustrated (flustered and frustrated); intertwingled (intermingled and intertwined). Try it with phrases, too: "I could do that with one eye tied behind my back!"

• Make up two lists of eight seemingly unrelated things with which both you and your child are familiar. The first list should contain objects: piano, dog, banana, stars, spatula, and so on. The second list should contain abstractions such as emotions or colors. Show the lists to your child and then cut up the paper so that each word is on its own slip. Fold the slips in half and put them in two separate hats. Each of you should take turns picking a word from each hat and then do the following:

Describe how the two items are the same;

Think of one word that describes them both at once;

Describe how the two items might be linked together, and make up a rhyme, a product, or a short narrative about them.

• Block out one of your child's senses such as sight, touch, or hearing. Depending upon the sense chosen, this can be done with blindfolds, ear or nose plugs (wadded tissue can be used), headphones, or gloves. Enlist your child's help in deciding how you're going to screen out the designated sense. Be sure the environment is a safe one, and that you or someone equally responsible will be there to assist your child if necessary. Prepare your child by explaining that this is a game. Set an agreed upon length of time for the exercise to run. Only children over the age of 5, who can clearly grasp the nature of the activity, should try it.

By restricting your child's hearing, or by inhibiting his sense of smell or touch, you force him to redraw mental and perceptual maps. As an analogy, imagine if the route you normally take to work were blocked. You would then have to find a new path. In so doing you would enlarge your sense of what's "out there," you would come to understand your old route in a different context, and you might discover certain responses or skills in yourself. This is what happens when your child suddenly has to experience his bedroom only through his hands, or navigate around the house blindfolded. He becomes aware of the smells he never noticed, or the tickings, hummings, buzzings, and squeakings he never heard. This repatterning facilitates right-left brain communication.

Many children who try this activity report a heightened appreciation of the importance of their senses, as well as amazement at how much of their environment they have been missing. (An added benefit of this exercise is that it increases children's sensitivity to some of the issues faced by the handicapped.)

• Ask your kids offbeat questions that make them think imaginatively by having to come up with all sorts of unusual and innovative ideas:

What would happen if it rained *up*?
What are you supposed to say when God sneezes?
What kind of weather is most like you?
Which weighs more: day or night?
Which takes up more space: A guilty conscience or a giraffe?

8

FLAP + TIRE + BEANSTALK = ?
ORIGINALITY

*T*he children we studied often flex their originality by standing apart from the pack. They wear their nonconformity proudly, displaying interests, tastes, beliefs, and even dress habits that others might label eccentric. We asked them why they did this. Their answers—"It's who I am"; "I'm not like everyone else"; "I enjoy being this way"—made it clear that they act this way, *not as a statement of rebellion, but as an expression of integrity and self-confidence.* At the same time that they declare their individuality, their empathic nature promotes tolerance of the opinions and behaviors of others. The ability to think with originality is critical to the creative process, and the ability to manifest creativity is crucial if a child is to respond capably to the people, problems, and responsibilities of life.

Three aspects of originality are particularly observable in creative, capable children:

- fluency
- remote associations
- preference for disorder.

FLUENCY

Fluency is the ability to produce a high quantity of ideas *without regard to their quality*. Photographers demonstrate the concept of fluency whenever they take hundreds of pictures (many of which may be of low quality) in order to come up with the one they need. Quantity often gives birth to quality. Edison tried more than two thousand combinations of metal before finding the right one for his first light bulb! Parents should encourage prolific thinking in their children. This may be done in a number of ways:

Brainstorm

When problems or opportunities present themselves—where to go for a family vacation; how to redecorate a child's bedroom; what to do about neglected responsibilities—engage the rules of brainstorming and cast a wide net for ideas. In a brainstorm, the goal is to generate a list of as many ideas as possible. No evaluation and judgment of any kind is allowed during this part of the process. Nothing inhibits a child's thinking or willingness to contribute more than critical comments like, "That wouldn't work"; "That would cost too much"; "Where did you get an idea like that!" After all ideas have been collected, the participants review them to narrow down the list. At this point, children are quite willing to recognize that certain ideas are too impractical or expensive. (See Chapter 13, "Problem-Solving," for more discussion of this technique.)

Don't Be Judgmental

Never scoff at the ideas of children. No matter how unrealistic or hastily conceived, for the child's age and experience they may be appropriate and admirable. When parents belittle their children's ideas, they belittle their children.

A much better approach for parents is to lead their children to consider for themselves the merits and/or consequences of the ideas they come up with. This can be done by asking open-ended questions that reflect your interest and model your willingness to be educated in new ways: "How would that work?"; "What do you think her reaction will be?"; "Have you figured out how much it will cost?"; "Did you consider other ways to do this?"

Questions should be asked in a neutral, nonjudgmental manner. Children sense if questions are merely disguised attacks. (Of course, the classic use of this method occurs when a child announces that he is going to run away: "Where will you go?"; "How will you get there?"; "Where will you sleep?"; "Who'll feed the dog?"; "I don't think they allow dogs on the bus. . . ." Rare is the child who, upon consideration of these logistical issues, won't elect to postpone running away until a more propitious occasion.)

If, after deep thought, your child insists on following an idea you consider to be silly or ill-advised, let her—provided, of course, that she doesn't endanger herself or others. In allowing your child to exercise her will, you offer her the chance to discover for herself the wisdom of her actions. If she should be proven "right," she will have learned the importance of believing in herself and standing up for her principles. If she should be proven "wrong," she will have learned it in the most valuable manner—through her own experience. You must be careful here not to project any hint of an "I-told-you-so" attitude. Your child knows you told her so. Far better that you emphasize what she can learn from the experience, and how she could choose to do things differently in the future.

Children who are fluent thinkers develop *intellectual playfulness*. They recognize that "silly" or farfetched ideas often trigger appropriate solutions to a problem. For example, one day a man was removing burrs from his pants after a walk through some fields and woods. He wondered if, by sewing some burrs to a piece of cloth, he could make a pocket that he could press onto his clothes anywhere he wanted one. This was a rather silly idea in that most of us tend to find pockets where we need them. Being an original thinker, however, this man pursued his notion and went on to invent synthetic burrs. He named his product "Velcro"! Another example of this process involved a group whose task was to think of the best way to discard automobile glass after the car had been crushed for recycling. One member of the group jokingly suggested that the glass be heated to a high temperature and tossed into a centrifuge so that it would come out looking like cotton candy. Someone else imagined that glass "cotton candy" could be molded—the result was fiber glass!

As they hold ideas up against the glare of reality, children hone their skills of self-evaluation and learn to avoid snap decisions. This shuttling between originality and practicality is a hallmark of creativity. This skill requires the ability to communicate swiftly between the left and right hemispheres of the brain (see Chapter 7).

REMOTE ASSOCIATIONS

The designer of the Remote Associates Test, Sarnoff Mednick, believes that creativity is the process by which ideas already in the mind are associated in unusual, original, and useful combinations. He calls these "remote associations." Every image or concept we have is linked with other images and concepts. These associations seem to be arranged in a list. At the top of the list are those concepts most closely linked to the original idea. As we move down the list, the strength of association becomes weaker. For example, if you were asked to say the first thing that comes into your mind when hearing the word *black*, you would possibly say "white," white being a strong associate of black. You would be less likely to have said "plague," or "shoes," or "Monday," or "sea"—all items which would be farther down on your list, if they are on it at all.

The Remote Associates Test was designed to measure one's ability to flexibly and freely associate ideas. Give it a try!

The Remote Associates Test
Instructions: In this test you are presented with three words and asked to find a fourth word which is related to the other three. Write this word in the space to the right. For example, what word do you think is related to these three?

     cookies   sixteen   heart   _____

The answer in this case is "sweet." Cookies are sweet; sweet is part of the phrase "sweet sixteen," and also part of the word "sweetheart."

Here is another example: poke   go   molasses

The correct answer is "slow." Now try these:

1.	flap	tire	beanstalk	_____
2.	mountain	up	school	_____
3.	package	cardboard	fist	_____
4.	surprise	line	birthday	_____
5.	madman	acorn	bolt	_____

6.	telephone	high	electric	_____
7.	hair	income	fish	_____
8.	cream	bulb	heavy	_____
9.	up	knife	Band-Aid	_____
10.	snow	wash	black	_____
11.	out	home	jail	_____
12.	slugger	belfry	ball	_____
13.	stage	game	actor	_____
14.	Roman	arithmetic	one	_____
15.	cat	color	holes	_____
16.	belle	snow	beach	_____

Answers on page 117.

High scores on this test have been found to correlate with high creativity. Children (who are at least 10 years old) of nurturing parents should also do well on this test, for they are able to see connections where others do not. They are able to cast broad and deep nets in their search for ideas. Thus, they generate more ideas (fluency), from more hidden recesses of the mind (remoteness). These two qualities, along with the one to be described below, are the bases of originality.

THE CHALLENGE OF CHAOS

Studies have shown that creative people have a "preference for disorder." This is not to say that all artists live in messy garrets, or that all inventors refuse to comb their hair. But generally speaking, *highly creative people enjoy the challenge of bringing order— their own order—out of disorder. They find a richness in chaos, and a pleasure in taming it.*

The issue of disorder may pose special problems for parents. Take your child's room, for example. If it's a disaster area, does this indicate that your child is a creative genius? Or just a slob? Or both?

The important issue for parents is to recognize that children have their own systems of order. So do adults. A computer-programming consultant we know was concerned that her son's inability to keep his room neat would affect his school performance.

"Well, how is he doing in school?" we asked.

"He gets B's. With the occasional A and C. But he starts high school in the fall."

"And?"

"And if he doesn't get better organized I don't see how he's going to manage."

"What does your office look like?"

"My office?" she laughed. "It looks like a cyclone hit it."

"Piles of paper?"

"Skyscrapers! Proposals, magazines, file folders." Our friend paused. "All right, all right. It looks like a mess, but I know where everything is. Is that your point?"

It is indeed. A child's room should be his castle. For many years, it is the one place in the world where a child can be master of his environment. It is there that he can work and play and stare at the ceiling, that he can host his friends and create a secure domain that answers to his rules, that says "This is me!" If disorder is a requisite of that domain, so be it.

"Yes, but what about teaching kids respect for property?"

"What about the virtues of being neat and organized and hanging clothes up in a closet?"

"What about *our* standards? If our kids are going to live in our house, they're going to obey our rules. . . ."

If you share these concerns, your parental reflexes are in proper working order. *But why bring a plague of unnecessary conflict upon your house?* Let your children keep their rooms the way they want. By respecting your child's domain, you model the respect you expect to receive for *your* domain—the rest of the house. Here's a double standard you can all get behind.

Consider the single father we know with three boys. He was telling us about the fight he has every morning to get his kids to make their beds.

"What does it matter whether they make their beds or not?" we asked.

He was taken aback. Finally, he answered. "So their rooms will look neat."

"Neatness is an adult value."

"Exactly. How are they going to learn it unless—"

"They'll learn it when it becomes important to them; when it engages *their* self-interest: maybe friends won't come over because their room is such a mess, maybe the dog chews up their science project, maybe their aesthetic needs change and they prefer to see the carpet instead of dirty clothes on the floor."

The father shook his head. "They have to learn to take care of their things."

"Ah, but that's a different issue."

"What do you mean?"

"Being neat isn't the same as being responsible. It's possible for a child to be messy without abusing his property, and for a neat child to be careless."

We went round and round for quite some time. This father came from a long line of bed-makers. To him, a neat room and made-up bed were associated with industry, virtue, and good hygiene.

Our point was not that he should give up teaching his children to respect authority, but that he created an unnecessary battle for himself every morning by insisting that his children adopt his aesthetic values. In the course of our discussion, he admitted that he was not personally inconvenienced by the disorder, and that he spent almost no time in his children's rooms (except when he read to them at bedtime and then the issue was moot; the beds in question being inhabited).

As an experiment, the father took our advice and announced to his sons that he would no longer insist that their beds be made. Immediately, the entire tenor of morning interactions changed. The tension that had come with dawn's early fight was eliminated—to everyone's benefit. Within weeks, the eldest boy began to make his bed on his own. Perhaps, now that there was no requirement to do so, leading to a power struggle (whose opinion is more important in this house?), he felt free to experiment with a new behavior.

Personality development is enhanced by control over one's environment. Many kids choose to exercise that control by maintaining their surroundings in an outwardly disordered fashion. If your child's room looks like the aftermath of Hurricane Zelda, the following guidelines can offer kids the freedom to grow within a framework that respects parental concerns:

• Allow your children their private disorder—as long as it's in their private space. It becomes public when it creeps, spills, or wafts into yours. (Generally, we find that creative disorder does not grow mold or overpower the house with "eau de locker room.")

• When not in their rooms, your children must respect the environmental standards you establish as the mortgagee. You have every right to insist that the living-room floor remain free of teen magazines, cassette tapes, and the debris of inconsideration.

• Doors were invented so parents wouldn't have to look at their children's rooms. So close them. Out of sight, out of mind.

• A child's room should adhere to minimum local building code standards (that is, unblocked egress), and health regulations (free of regenerative food mutations).

• Sometimes disorder is not a manifestation of the creative spirit. Instead, it is a statement that better storage systems are needed. Talk with your kids about their rooms. Would it help if they had more shelf space, a bigger desk, a file cabinet, a huge trunk, or a closet annex?

Disorder and abuse of belongings are two separate issues, but often they become confused. We would never advocate that parents happily tolerate their children's mistreatment of property. Fortunately, a system of discipline exists to deal very effectively with this issue (as well as almost all others)—a system so elegant, easy, and just that we're amazed it's so rarely used! It is called "logical consequences." We believe it is the best thing parents can give their children after love, respect, and that recent hallmark of modern child-rearing, KA-WALITY TIME.

The easiest way to describe this approach to discipline is by comparing it to punishment. Punishments humiliate and frighten. They emphasize the parent's power and the child's defenselessness. They are based on threats and revenge. Punishments make kids feel hurt, guilty, unloved, and bad. They usually have little to do with the specifics of a child's "crime." What is the connection, for example, between hitting a sibling and being grounded? Lying and getting spanked? Forgetting one's chores and not being allowed to go to a party?

These kinds of punishments can actually engender further rebellion and dishonesty. Ultimately, they don't work. Sooner or
later, a child with backbone will call his parent's bluff. He storms
out of the house in spite of being grounded; he hits back; he
sneaks out to the party. Escalating punishments can be met with
escalating defiance. Communication and trust suffer a meltdown
and the nuclear family is destroyed.

Unlike punishments, which place responsibility for enforcing
the child's good behavior on the parent, *logical consequences
hold the child responsible*. They present the child with the natural,
appropriate consequences for his actions. They teach the child his
error without assaulting his self-esteem. Their purpose is restor-
ative: to undo damage, to prevent future occurrences, to soothe
hurt feelings. This method is a major part of nurturing parenting.

The chart below illustrates the differences between punishments and logical consequences:

Logical consequences don't mean that a child has gotten away
with anything; there's nothing "permissive" about them. They

CRIME AND PUNISHMENT (AND LOGICAL CONSEQUENCES)

The Child's Crime	A Punishment	vs. A Logical Consequence
Breaks the porch screen in a fit of anger.	No TV for a week.	Fixing the screen himself and having to pay for the materials.
Hits his little sister.	Gets spanked so he'll understand it's wrong to hit anyone.	Must do something nice for her—take her skating or to a movie.
Doesn't do his chores.	Not allowed to go to school dance.	Must reimburse parents for the cost of teenager they've hired to do chores in his place.

present the child with options, not threats. If she *chooses* to ignore a curfew, she will not be able to stay out late. If he *chooses* to drive recklessly, he won't be able to use the car.

Logical consequences are a good way for parents to deal with destructive disorder. Why rant and rave when you can simply allow your child to be confronted with the consequences of her actions? If disorder leads to possessions being broken, your child loses the use of them. You are not beholden to replace or repair them. That is her responsibility. If clothes become torn or dirty beyond normal wear and tear due to their being tossed on the floor, your child can quickly learn how to sew and do laundry. This approach presents the child with a system in which *she* holds the cards. You are not the agent of punishment. You are a reminder of reality.

Disorder and Life Management

A number of years ago, one of us spent the summer living in the house of a famous professor. He was known throughout the world for the originality and brilliance of his contributions to psychology. The extent of his influence was proof of his creativity.

However, the disorder in his practical life was another matter. It was not unusual to come into the kitchen to find smoke pouring out of the toaster, the professor sitting oblivious six feet away. He often forgot to extinguish matches; on several occasions fires had to be put out in wastebaskets. Car doors and windows were left wide open in thunderstorms; the professor was forever coming home in the middle of the day in search of misplaced papers; the phone often rang with inquiries from others as to the professor's whereabouts. He was supposed to have been at an appointment an hour ago.

This is an example of disorderliness in the area of life management. We would hesitate to call it a preference for disorder in that there is probably little choice involved. (Who would choose to leave a trail of bonfires throughout one's house?) But the image of the absentminded professor, so involved with the peregrinations of the mind as to be oblivious to the world around him, would not have stuck if there weren't some truth to it. Kids have a term for people like these: space cadets.

If your child orbits the earth in a cloud of disorder, the important thing is to sense whether it is productive or destructive to the management of his life. What does it matter if he has no assignment notebook or appointments calendar, so long as he meets his responsibilities? The filing system for his life doesn't have to be comprehensible to you—only to him.

However, if the mechanics of his life are out of control, if he constantly loses, breaks, and forgets things, if his assignments are late and his library books overdue, if he misses appointments and overlooks commitments, if his friends complain about his flakiness, then he has not found workable systems for ordering the practical world. He needs your help.

These ideas will help kids minimize the destructive effects of disorder in the management of their lives:

• Explore through discussion the possibility that your child's difficulties are due to having taken on too much—he may be swamped by schoolwork, lessons, sports, social obligations, and outside interests. It's not so much that *he's* disordered as it is that the system is strained beyond capacity. If this is the case, help your child find ways to reduce his responsibilities by dropping a course, rescheduling a deadline, postponing an activity, or asking for assistance from a friend. Recognizing one's limits is not an act of weakness, it is an act of responsibility.

• Let your child experience the consequences of her actions. Don't "enable" disorganization by covering up for her mistakes or rescuing her from situations she has created for herself and is perfectly capable of handling. Make *her* smooth ruffled feathers, pay library fines, and reschedule missed dental appointments. This is not a hardhearted lack of support. It is an expression of respect for your child's autonomy, and faith in her ability to manage her affairs. When your child is not capable of negotiating the situation herself—she is experiencing a crisis, or safety is at issue, or the powers that be have come crashing down unfairly—it is important to be aware of this and step in. Signs that your child is in over her head can be: sleeplessness or nightmares, depression (listlessness, feelings of hopelessness), unreasonable fears, avoidance, or other uncharacteristic behaviors and attitudes.

• Create and display personal and family schedules. All appointments and commitments should be listed. Each day your child can check her own calendar and the family calendar to see what's on the docket. Even children who are too young to read and write can do this by tacking up pictures cut out from magazines.

• Wonderful computer programs exist to help people order their lives. Your child should learn how to use one (on a school computer if you don't have one). It will remind him of obligations, deadlines, finances, special events—anything and everything.

• Make contracts. Some kids enjoy the formality of writing down the precise conditions that underlie their responsibilities and agreements. This works best within families, but kids—particularly when they need to dig out from under—have used this technique successfully with teachers in school. Teachers respect the initiative shown by a child who is willing to work out an agreement such as this, and children learn how to negotiate solutions, not fight about them or be nagged into stubborn resistance. (It's a bit like working out a payment schedule with your creditors.)

• Encourage your child to create a support system of reminders for herself. As long as she takes responsibility for its working (or not working), there's nothing wrong with enlisting the help of others to steer a more orderly and responsible course through life. (It's like remembering to set an alarm clock—the clock does the reminding, but you're still responsible for setting the alarm and getting up once it's gone off.)

Originality is a hallmark of the "can-do" kids we studied. It allows them to generate many ideas, to look for new concepts in remote and unlikely places, and to enjoy the disorder that typically accompanies the creative process. One of the things that most often truncates the range of a child's originality is gender-role stereotyping. The child learns to accept, reject, or repress ideas based on images of what is properly "masculine" or "feminine." Nurturing parenting is particularly successful in freeing children from these restrictions. Not surprisingly, the children in our study often cross gender barriers in their interests and emotional expression. This trait, known as *androgyny*, is associated with empathy, responsibility, and high creativity, and can be fostered in many ways by nurturing parents. We will have much more to say about gender roles and the nurturing of androgyny in the next chapter.

ACTIVITIES TO NURTURE THE TRAIT OF ORIGINALITY

BUILDING YOUR OWN NEST

Materials: blankets, sheets, scarves, string, sticks, pillows, leaves, etcetera.

Take your child for a walk in the woods or a city park. Ask him to help you find a bird's nest by watching where the birds fly. Once a nest is spotted (even pigeons make nests of some sort—squirrels' nests might also be observed), look closely at it. Don't touch it, though—its owners will abandon it if they smell your hand.

Talk with your child about how birds build their nests out of things that they gather in their travels. Ask him what he thinks birds especially like to use to make nests.

When you return home, ask your child to imagine what he could use to build a "nest" that would be just right for him. What textures would he most like to feel? What colors would he most like to see? After he has imagined his nest, encourage him to build it (whether indoors or outdoors will depend on his choice of materials). Once your child has created his nest, ask him to curl up in it and describe what he likes about being there. Ask him what he thinks birds might like best about his nest.

Extensions:

Have your child stock or modify his nest according to various conditions you set, such as: it's going to rain for the next three days; his nest is going to fly around the world; his best friend is going to spend the night; an army of grasshoppers is going to attack sometime that afternoon.

Forts, treehouses, and cardboard cottages are wonderful "nests" for older children. Scavenge for building materials and let them go to it (with appropriate supervision, of course), either in the backyard or basement. All kids should have a "womb" of their own.

OTHER ACTIVITIES

The following activities not only promote original thinking, but they are also good responses to that perennial complaint, "There's nothing to do!":

• Give your child ten colored pipe cleaners. Tell him he can make anything he chooses as long as it is one object. When he has finished, give him ten more and tell him to make an object completely different from the first.

• Create a sound sculpture. String a clothesline between two trees or posts. Have your child affix items to the line that will make interesting sounds in the wind when struck by other objects.

• Make a giant soap bubble blower from a coffee can opened at both ends and a large balloon. Here's how. Hold the balloon by the stem and cut off the bottom half. (This may be discarded.) Now stretch the wide, cut end of the balloon half over one end of the can. Dip the other end of the can in soapy water, and blow gently on the balloon stem. Tell your child to go for a mental ride in the bubble and to describe what she sees.

• In a bucket or old paint can, collect some water filled with lovely slimy wildlife from a swamp or pond. Ask your child to predict what you will find in the water when you take a closer look. Then, using a magnifying glass or microscope, explore the water. When you have finished, be sure to return the wildlife to its natural habitat.

• Present your child with the cleaned, dried, and disassembled bones of a chicken or turkey (use vinegar to clean the bones). The disassembled bones are a puzzle with infinite solutions: the child's task is to create something new with them. (Glue, clay, string, tape, pins, putty, and even chewing gum can be used to connect the bones.) Of course it is possible to try to remake the chicken or turkey, but even more imagination is needed to make some other kind of animal or structure. Some kids have even made marionettes! After the bones are assembled, the skeleton can be decorated with papier-mâché, paints, feathers, leaves, "fur," etcetera.

• Ask your child to tell you how the world would be different if there were dinosaurs in it (or space people, or money trees, or rivers instead of streets).

• Present your child with a paper bag full of odds and ends which she'll use to create a sculpture.

• Give your child a felt-tip pen or crayon. Challenge him to write a message or make a drawing on a material other than paper. The idea is to come up with as many substitutes as possible: a leaf, eggshells, a banana peel, stones, and so on. Establish ground rules so he'll understand that only materials that cannot be damaged are allowed; walls, car doors, clothing, or other people's belongings are all off limits.

• Now that you've worked hard to teach your child how to set the table correctly, pose the following challenge to him: "How many ways can you think of to set the table? Each night, show us a different way." A chore will be turned into a funny ritual for the entire (courageous) family. Delight as your child hides the silverware under the napkins one evening, gives Daddy three knives the next, makes sunray designs out of spoons, places the empty cups upside down....

• Pack your sack! Tell your child to go through the house collecting everything he'll need for a trip to the moon, the desert, or the bottom of the sea. Have him tell you what he selected and why.

• Next time your child says, "What can I do?" suggest that she go on a scavenger hunt around the house to find all the different things that come in pairs (hinges on a cabinet door), threes (legs on a music stand), and fours (burners on a stove). This activity can be varied by having her look for all the items that meet other criteria: things that float on water, things you'd never give to a baby, things that do not have a front or a back, and so on.

• Provide your child with a notebook. At the top of each page write a question to answer that starts with the words, "What are all the ways....?" For example:

"What are all the ways to send a message from San Francisco to New York?"

"What are all the ways to get across a creek in the woods?"

"What are all the ways to take a dog on a bus without anyone knowing?"

This activity works well with small groups. Have each child create a notebook to swap with someone else.

• Pick a section in your yard where weeds are growing. With four sticks and a string, mark off a square one yard on each side. Ask your child to imagine what might be living in that square. Then, with a scissors or pair of garden clippers, cut down all the vegetation in the square so that it is as close to the ground as you can get, and take a look.

• Suggest some object (the stripes on a zebra, a tail on a horse, thorns on a rosebush) or some circumstance (the man in the moon, clouds floating in the sky, cats but not dogs being able to climb trees). Ask your child to think of as many possible explanations for these things as she can.

• Suggest that your child try to describe all the things for which the number 10 stands. Here are some examples: $5 + 5$; $13 - 3$; $4 + 2 + 1 + 1 + 1 + 1$; a decade; five sets of twins, the number of eggs left in a carton when two of the eggs have been eaten.

• Challenge your child to think of:

   all the names she can for the word *road* (lane, thoroughfare, boulevard, parkway);

   all the different kinds of water (rainwater, bathwater, water you can lead a horse to but you can't make it drink);

   all the ways water exists in nature (lake, ocean, pond, stream, spring, oasis, inlet, bay, etcetera);

   all things that roll on wheels (extra credit for things people don't generally ride in: vacuum cleaners, suitcases, wheelbarrows, push lawn mowers).

• The goal of this game is to think of as many unusual-but-appropriate names as possible for people in different jobs. For example, someone who sells eyeglasses might be named "Iris Pupil"; an auto mechanic, "Jack Itup"; a professor at Harvard, "Ivy League"; a bank teller, "Bill Changer."

• The next time you go food shopping, instead of putting away the groceries immediately, see how many different systems your child can think of to organize them. Ask him to do so and to see if you can guess the method behind his madness. Examples: according to package size or shape; according to texture of product (such as liquids, gooey things, grainy things, spongy things); according to function (such as "bread spreads," sauces, things you mix in liquids); according to name characteristics (for instance, alphabetized storage, syllabic storage); according to source of product (animals, trees, earth, water, and so on).

• Challenge your child to build a centerpiece for the dining-room table designed to provoke conversation about a certain subject of her choosing: sports, China, volcanoes, bird-watching, etcetera. The tricky part of this is that the centerpiece should provoke the conversation without being the focus of the conversation.

• Give your child the Remote Associates Test to take. (She should be at least 10 years old. See page 104 for instructions) Once she's finished, talk about the idea of remote associations. Ask her to think of ways in which remote associations can be valuable: for example, when writing poetry, doing a crossword puzzle, solving a problem. Then, suggest that she make up her own Remote Associates Test for her friends or family to take. Working the process backwards is an excellent way to foster originality. The brain hemispheres also get an excellent workout as both convergent and divergent thinking are needed for this activity! (See Chapter 7.)

Answers to the Remote Associates Test

1. jack	9. cut
2. grade, high	10 white
3. box	11. house
4. party	12. bat
5. nut	13. play
6. wire	14. numeral
7. net	15. black
8. light	16. ball

9

SUGAR AND SPICE AND PUPPY DOGS' TAILS: ANDROGYNY

*B*etween 1946 and 1975, psychologist Anne Roe conducted a number of studies involving artists and scientists. In this research, she explored the relationship between "gender role identification" and creativity. It was found that people with ordinary levels of creative ability tend to conform to those stereotypical characteristics identified as male or female. Highly creative people, however, were found to be androgynous; that is, they have greater than average male *and* female elements in their personalities.

In an extensive 1978 study of highly successful male architects, MacKinnon reported that these individuals showed markedly greater levels of androgyny than did people of ordinary ability:

> *The evidence is clear. The more creative a [man] is, the more he reveals an openness to his own feelings and emotions, a sensitive intellect and understanding self-awareness, and wide-ranging interests including many which in the American culture are thought of as feminine. In the realm of sexual identification and interest, our creative subjects appear to give more expression to the feminine side of their nature than do less creative persons. In the language of the Swiss psychologist Carl Jung, creative persons are not so completely identified with their masculine persona roles as to blind themselves to or to deny expression to the more feminine traits of the anima [Jung's term for the unconscious female nature].*

In a 1970 study of women mathematicians, Helson and Crutchfield found similar indications that those who are most successful tend to be more androgynous than those of more ordinary ability. Why should this be so? The likely explanation is that the ability to produce highly innovative ideas in mathematics requires individuals of either gender to have some of the qualities traditionally identified with the opposite gender. Creative males need to be empathetic and intuitive; creative females need to be assertive and "unemotional" in order to promote and defend their ideas in a critical world.

But parents needn't worry. Androgyny is not the same as cross-gender behavior, nor is it simply the midpoint between the two poles of masculinity and femininity. Children who are androgynous are not *less* masculine if they are boys, or *less* feminine if they are girls, than other children. They retain the characteristics of their own gender. They differ, though, in that their personalities are enriched with *additional* interests and attitudes typically associated with the opposite sex. Thus, androgyny is more expansive than either of the more traditional roles. As such, it frees the individual from the constraints placed by gender stereotyping upon thought, feeling, and action.

Rigid gender roles are costly to the personality—they're really a form of being stimulus-bound (see Chapter 5). Such rigidity frequently causes children to discard interests and suppress feelings in order to conform to gender-role "norms." Numerous studies indicate that young children are naturally androgynous but that they learn well-established gender roles by the end of their second year. This learning quickly restricts the options of the average child. The resulting conflicts can inhibit personality development as kids are forced to overrule their natural impulses. Androgynous children, however, with an expanded repertoire of options, are more likely to "find" or become themselves.

How does one recognize androgyny in children? Androgynous boys often reveal a gentle side to their nature. They readily display their emotions and are sensitive and empathic toward the needs and feelings of others. In addition to engaging in rough-and-tumble boyhood activities, these boys may have other interests considered less typical of their gender: art, cooking, baby-sitting, keeping a diary. They may also enjoy the friendship of girls during the traditionally "anti-girl" latency years.

Androgynous girls can be scrappy and competitive, eager to take on leadership roles. They are unfazed by physical aggression and may participate in "boys' " contact sports such as basketball and soccer. Their androgyny allows them to have broad interests—outer space, cars, how things work. Because they are unencumbered by gender-role stereotyping, they see themselves as having a greater variety of opportunities. Thus, their plans for the future are less restricted than those of other girls.

For the majority of children, gender differences take hold and limit options because most parents communicate, both consciously and unconsciously, the attitudes with which they were raised. Thus, the first thing parents must do to nurture androgyny is to take stock of their own feelings. The best way to do this is by asking oneself a number of questions:

> Was I taught at an early age that boys don't cry and girls don't yell?
>
> Did my parents applaud or discourage my behavior on the basis of gender-role stereotypes?
>
> Was I encouraged to pursue interests even when those interests "belonged" to the opposite gender?
>
> Did I go to a school where boys took shop and girls took home ec?
>
> Did I ever hide or abandon an interest because I was afraid of being teased about it?
>
> Was my career choice influenced by gender-role stereotyping?
>
> Have I ever said to my daughter, "Don't do that, it isn't ladylike?"
>
> How would I react if my 4-year-old son asked for a Barbie doll, or if my 4-year-old daughter asked for a Rambo doll?
>
> Do I believe that blue is for boys and pink is for girls?
>
> Would I discourage my son from playing the harp or taking ballet lessons?
>
> If my daughter were prohibited from playing on a school sports team because she was a girl, what would I do?
>
> Do my spouse and I communicate gender-role stereotypes through the roles we take in our household? For exam-

ple, which one of us cleans, cooks, cuts the lawn, fixes the
car, etcetera?

Before I had children, did I have visions of what I hoped my
son and/or daughter would be like? Did I have different
visions for a son than for a daughter? Were these influenced by sex-role stereotyping?

Am I disappointed if my children don't meet all of society's
expectations for their gender? Am I disappointed if my
children *do* meet all of society's expectations for their
gender? (We know parents who are terribly upset when,
in spite of all their efforts toward gender-role neutrality,
their little boys seek out toy guns and their little girls ask
for kitchen sets and play "housewife.")

Have I ever thought that my son is too "sensitive"? Or that my
daughter is too "tough"?

Have my spouse and I talked about the impact of gender roles
on our own childhood and adult lives? Did we formulate
a position on the issue of gender roles when we discussed how we wanted to raise our own children?

Sex-role stereotyping has diminished in the wake of the fem-
inist movement, but it would be a mistake to assume that sex-role
stereotyping is a thing of the past. Children continue to receive
direct and indirect messages from their peers, parents, and culture that define behavior in terms of gender. This can be seen in
one of the findings of a recent survey conducted by Alex Packer.
Approximately 300 children ages 11 to 15 were asked the following question: "Has anyone ever told you that you can't or shouldn't
do something just because you're a boy or a girl?"

Nearly half (47 percent) of the youngsters answered "Yes."

Moreover, girls responded "Yes" to this question by an almost
three-to-one margin over boys (67 to 23 percent)! The disparity is
even greater when we consider that many of the boys who answered "Yes" cite injunctions that are quite proper, and not representative of sex-role stereotyping:

They said I couldn't go into the girl's bathroom;
I was told to stay out of the girls' locker room;
They said I couldn't have a baby.

Virtually all of the girls, however, relate incidents that are clear examples of gender-based discrimination. A sampling of these comments, from both boys and girls, illustrates many of the attitudes and experiences likely to extinguish androgyny.

"What was it you were told you can't or shouldn't do just because you're a *boy*?"

> Cook. I always am willing to cook at home and I feel my mom never lets me because she thinks boys don't know how.
> My father said I couldn't get my ear pierced because I was a boy.
> They said I couldn't jump rope.
> They said I couldn't baby-sit for someone. ("So what did you do?" the survey asked.) I held a formal protest!

What was it you were told you can't or shouldn't do just because you're a *girl*?

> That I couldn't collect baseball cards.
> That I couldn't play poker.
> That girls should stay in the house and not ride skateboards.
> That girls don't play with army dolls or G.I. Joes. ("So what did you do?") I beat up my brother and played with his toys.
> They said I couldn't stay out late but that my brother could, because he was a boy.
> My mother says I have to do more housework than my brother because I'm a girl.
> They said that I couldn't ever climb trees because I was a girl and girls are supposed to be more intelligent than that. ("So what did you do?") Well, I did climb that tree and now they think I'm the best. Now I dare *them* to do things.
> Mr.—— thinks girls should not play football and ruin our wonderful legs.
> Whenever I volunteer to carry a heavy item, my teachers say I can't do it because I'm a girl.
> They said I couldn't ask a boy out because I was a girl, and that girls didn't do that. It was the boy's job. ("So what did you

do?") I asked the boy out because I didn't agree with that
theory, and everything turned out great.

They said I shouldn't play baseball or football. I said girls can
do anything boys can do, so shut up or I'll show you
something I'm good at!

While these comments make it evident that sex stereotyping is
alive and well, the feisty responses many children express give
reason to hope for sex stereotyping's continued decline. They also
point the way to the most important things parents can do to
nurture their children's androgyny:

• Go to bat for your children if they are the victims of gender-
role stereotyping. For children who are equipped to fight their
own battles, this usually means talking, listening, and providing
emotional support for whatever course of action your kids choose.
Sometimes, however, being a victim of stereotyping leaves children feeling stuck and unable to see a way out. Here you have to
step in and explain to them how they have been victimized, and
what their options are. You may also have to intercede with school
officials or coaches, or even obtain legal assistance.

• Be alert to your own attitudes and prejudices regarding gender roles. If you treat your sons and daughters differently, is it
because of *their* preferences or *yours*? Do you present them both
with similar options, or do you tend to think in terms of boys'
interests and girls' interests, boys' behavior and girls' behavior? Of
course, it's fine if you never play catch with your daughter—
provided it's *her* choice—*and*, you provided her with as many
opportunities as you did your son to develop an interest in this
activity. (By the way, is it just Dad who plays catch with the kids?)
You can see how subtle sex-role stereotyping can be. Even the
most open-minded parents may unwittingly communicate gender-
defined messages to their children. For example, if your son skins
his knee, do you expect his tears to dry faster than if your daughter skins hers? Do you say to him, "It's just a little scratch. You're
a big boy; let's be brave and wipe away those tears"; while to your
daughter you say, "Oh, you poor little baby, I know how much it
hurts, maybe next time you shouldn't be so rough."

• Show interest in and enthusiasm for your child's pursuits

regardless of their sex-stereotyped gender assignation. Boys will sense quickly whether their fathers disapprove of poetry-writing; girls will pick up the ways their parents try to discourage fort-building or rough-housing.

Some parents find themselves uncomfortable with the concept of androgyny because they assume—wrongly—that androgyny implies a "weakened" or confused sexual identity. If a boy is gentle and sensitive, the unexpressed fear is that he might grow up to become homosexual. Thus, any tendencies in androgynous directions must be stamped out early. This, in our opinion, is macho ado about nothing; androgyny and sexual orientation are not causally related. The squelching of so-called "feminine" interests in boys, or "masculine" interests in girls, will not alter sexual orientation. It *will* inhibit healthy personality development, however, and this is why nurturing parents make every effort to support their children's interests and feelings—without regard to the gender of the child or the "gender" of the interest itself.

To deny children the expression of feelings and interests on the basis of their gender is as arbitrary as denying them on the basis of hair color or first name. Imagine how people would react if the arbiters of society suddenly dictated that only redheads could pursue the sciences, or that only children whose names begin with the letters A through M could cry. Yet sex-role stereotyping does the same thing.

By expanding the range of your child's feelings, interests, and behaviors, androgyny expands your child's future. The fewer role boundaries your child believes in, the more creative and empathetic he or she can be. The more empathetic your child is, the more he or she can learn from people and experience different kinds of friendships (not only across gender, but across race, age, culture, and so on). By increasing the spectrum of experience available to a child, it feeds the child's creativity and empathy; this nourishes new options and relationships which in turn reinforce androgyny, enriching the child's life even more. This is why nurturing parents recognize that protecting and fostering the innate androgyny of their children is one of the most important things they can do to promote their child's full and healthy growth.

ACTIVITIES TO FOSTER THE TRAIT OF ANDROGYNY

Each of the activities that follows has three goals:

- to heighten your child's awareness of the stereotypes he holds of each gender;
- to challenge these biases and make him understand how and why they are unrealistic;
- to encourage him to react emotionally as well as cognitively to the inherent unfairness of gender-based stereotyping.

Achieving these goals will require your help. You will need to discuss each of the stereotypes that emerge through the activity so that your child can recognize the assumptions she makes about sex roles and use the knowledge gained to reach more open-minded conclusions.

Before starting these activities, help your child get into the right spirit by asking how she would react if the following things were to occur in her school:

- Only left-handed children were allowed to get A's.
- The teacher answered the questions only of blue-eyed kids.
- Boys could go to the bathroom only in the morning, girls in the afternoon.

Perceiving the outrageousness of these conditions will put children in the right frame of mind to tackle the activities below.

STOP THAT STEREOTYPING

Materials: pencil and paper.

Read the following description to a group of three or more children. Their job is to figure out if the person is a man or a woman simply by asking questions. (No questions relating to obvious physical characteristics are allowed.)

Imagine a person named Chris, who is taller than average, and rather thin. Chris has blue eyes and black hair of medium length. Chris is a good athlete and is especially good at running, skating, and swimming. Although a little on the shy side, Chris is quite popular and is readily accepted by most groups. Chris is of average intelligence, not too good at writing, but above average in math.

The two traits that stand out most about Chris are responsibility and empathy. People often say, "If you need someone to do a good job for you, someone you can trust, Chris is the person for you!" "If you are feeling upset, talking to Chris will make you feel a lot better!"

The assumptions kids make about gender roles become clear as they pose their questions: "Does Chris like to cook?" "Does Chris cry a lot?" "Would Chris play with toy soldiers?" Keep a running list of the questions asked so that you can discuss the underlying assumptions later. Encourage friendly arguments. This is where the learning takes place. The ultimate goal, of course, is to help the children realize that there are virtually *no* questions that can indisputably determine Chris's gender. Can *you* think of any?

Extensions:

Different children can write their own descriptions for presentation to the group. To be sure the gender of the character remains constant while questions are being asked, the presenter should write *male* or *female* on a separate slip of paper at the beginning of the game.

Older children can use their knowledge of sex-role stereotypes to deliberately embed their descriptions with tricky details, for instance, Chris shaves the hair on his or her legs once a week (Aha! Chris has to be a girl—no, Chris turns out to be a boy on the swim team); Chris wears a suit to work every day (Aha! Chris must be a man—no, Chris is a female diving instructor who wears a bathing suit to her job!).

JACK AND JILL IN THE BOX

Materials: one purse, into which you have put "male" items which could be used by females: a pipe, a screwdriver, a baseball, etcetera.; one briefcase into which you have put "female" items which could be used by males: a pocket mirror, a jar of hand lotion, a recipe, a set of knitting needles; one box into which you have placed objects that are as likely to be used by one gender as another; pens, bus tokens, ticket stubs, Scotch tape, a lemon drop, a bar of soap.

This activity fosters androgyny from another angle—by examining the gender assumptions children make about objects. Have your child open the purse, explore the items, and then give you a description of the person to whom they belong. Then ask her to do the same with the briefcase and the box. Younger children usually have a lot of difficulty with this task due to the conflict between the objects and their container, and, in the case of the box, the lack of cues. Even older children often experience considerable confusion. This presents you with an excellent opportunity to explain the concept of gender roles. It is through the discussion that these activities trigger that you can help your kids develop more stimulus and functional freedom with respect to gender roles, and this, of course, is the essence of androgyny.

OTHER ACTIVITIES

• This activity is designed to foster a deeper awareness of what roles society assigns to males and females. Start by asking your child to consider what it means to be male and what it means to be female, by trying to answer these questions:

Are there some things only men can or should do?
Are there some things only women can or should do?
At what kinds of things are people naturally better because of their gender?
Besides physical differences, what distinguishes men from women?
Are there reasons why we need men and women to be different?

You might encourage your child to obtain additional perspectives by discussing these issues with his peers.

Next, suggest that your child launch his own investigation of gender differences. As him to think about an environment where he can observe the behavior of men and women. A shopping mall is a wonderful place for such a study. Prior to observing, have your child develop hypotheses about what men and women do in that setting: for example, "There'll be more women than men;" "Women will come with children, men won't;" "More men than women will appear to be waiting," and so on. At the mall, he should keep a record of his discoveries, such as:

> Which gender is most likely to enter which type of store?
> What are the differences in purchases between males and females?
> What kinds of questions do women versus men ask sales clerks in a particular store?
> Are men and women equally likely to have children with them?

The variety of questions your child might pursue is obviously quite extensive. After your child has completed his research, discuss his findings with him and compare them to his expectations. Does this study make him rethink any of his answers to the questions he first considered? Does he think what he saw is an accurate reflection of gender differences or gender stereotyping? With humor and gentleness, back your child into the corners to which gender-stereotyping often leads. Help him to see that his hypotheses and observations may be based upon gender-role biases, or their effects in our society. For example, if your child predicted that more women than men would enter the supermarket, on what did he base this hypothesis? Is it because women are *supposed* to do the cooking and food shopping? Or because women have more free time? Or women are better at grocery shopping? Or does it simply reflect the existing roles and biases prevalent in our culture?

• After reading a favorite story, go back to the start of the story and tell your child that this time you and she are going to tell the story in a new way. Suggest that she tell the story from a cross-gender perspective (Goldilocks becomes a boy; Peter and the Wolf becomes Patty and the Wolf; Cinderella and her stepsisters become boys—and it's *Princess* Charming who does the saving!). If the story contains animals that seem to have no gender, ask your child if she thinks they are boys or girls and why. "The leopard is a boy because he hunts and is brave"; "The kangaroo must be a girl because she sings to her babies every night." Challenge these reasons if they show evidence of gender stereotyping. Help your child see that heroism, cowardice, timidity, bravery, and meanness needn't be masculine or feminine.

• Talk with your child about what it might be like to be the opposite sex for a day. Discuss what things she thinks she would still like to do, and what new things she would enjoy doing if she were a boy. Ask her if she could do these things anyway—as a girl. If she says yes, give her the support she may need to try them out. If she says no, find out why not. She'll probably say that people would tease her, or that the boys would laugh, or that her friends would think she was weird. She may even say that girls don't do that sort of thing. Each of these reasons offers a wonderful opportunity to discuss the way other people's expectations and gender stereotyping influence our behavior.

• Select a list of jobs usually done by males or females, and ask a small group of kids to tell you which gender does each job best. Ask them to explain their judgments. In some cases, they may make sense. In others, they may reflect stereotypes. Ask the group if they agree or disagree with each person's reasoning. This will poke holes in gender biases and reveal how few jobs there are that are legitimately "male" or "female." (Come to think of it, what are they?)

• Ask your child to try to list as many ways as he can describing how his life would be different if he were a member of the opposite sex. Then suggest that he show his list to a girl who is similar in age and see if she agrees with it. Also invite her to make her own list and share it with him.

• Pose the following riddle to your child:

A boy is rushed to the hospital following a car crash in which his father is killed. The boy is wheeled into the emergency operating room where a surgeon is ready to operate. "Oh my God!" the surgeon exclaims—for the child is the surgeon's son. How can this be?

Gender stereotyping may cause many children to ponder this question for a long time before coming up with a solution. Children with an androgynous outlook (stimulus freedom can be helpful, too) will quickly realize that the riddle makes perfect sense: the surgeon is the boy's mother!

10

CALM NERVES,
A FOCUSED MIND,
AND A PLAN:
SELF-CONTROL

*S*elf-control is a constant issue in our lives. Every day we use it, think about it, and probably wish we had more of it. Many people engage in grim, ongoing battles with self-control, their sense of self-worth under continual attack: If only I had more self-control I would . . .

> . . . lose weight
> . . . start exercising
> . . . stop smoking
> . . . study harder
> . . . put a lid on my temper.

Self-control affects our self-esteem, our relationships, and our potential for growth and achievement. It is something that nurturing parents model and value.

Nurturing parents believe that self-control can be fostered. They have faith in their children's ability to act wisely and constructively. Every time they encourage their children to anticipate the consequences of their actions, to assume responsibility, and to make decisions, they help them to practice and exercise self-control.

Children with self-control are in the driver's seat. From there, they command two different types of self-control. First is the immediate control that essentially keeps the car safely on the road at any given moment: the quick adjustments of steering, the touch of the brake, the singing of a song to stay alert. In the child's daily life, this is the type of self-control used to conform to appropriate standards of behavior (raising one's hand in class, withholding hurtful remarks), to march through the discipline of a schedule or meet a deadline, and to fulfill or resist immediate wants and needs.

While this "short-range" control keeps the car safely on the road, it is the second type of self-control that keeps the car going over the long haul, that has the larger destination in mind: where will I be at the end of the day? At the end of the year? If I keep traveling, where will I be five years from now? Ten years from now?

These two types of control are mutually inclusive: where we will be one year from now is going to be influenced by our impulse control in the moment; how we control ourselves in the moment is going to be influenced by where we want to be one year from now. Keeping these two forces in balance is one of the most difficult things a human being can do. When they are out of balance, the person is like a car out of tune: inefficient and prone to stalling. When they are in balance, the person is a powerful, virtually unstoppable force, capable of going almost anywhere and doing almost anything.

One can think of maturity as the increasing ability to use long-term goals to govern short-term behavior. Most people learn enough self-control to conform to society's laws, to hold down a job, and to fulfill their important responsibilities to others. Yet many of these people still trudge through life with the feeling that they are *not* in control. They feel plagued by bad habits and a lack of willpower. Long-term goals remain elusive or unidentified. Self-esteem is weakened by an inability to do the things their mind tells them they should or want to do. These people have enough self-control to stay on the road. But they go where the roads take them. Nurtured kids have both kinds of control. They choose their own roads.

This second type of self-control is hard for many people to come by. It is motivated by passion, self-confidence, and a sense of self-worth. It requires insight, faith, and a vision of a compelling future. It is this self-control that sets the children in our study apart from most of their peers.

We all know people who appear to lead lives of great discipline and accomplishment but who, underneath the surface, are driven and obsessed. Their self-control is not inspired by passion; rather, it is pushed by doubts and demons. Our concern, of course, is with the positive forms of self-control that nurturing parents foster.

The self-control that enables nurtured kids to reach distant and fabulous goals springs from three sources:

- a calm nervous system
- a passion and a plan
- a focused, faithful mind

A CALM NERVOUS SYSTEM

Agitation is a great foe of self-control. When we're all worked up about something, when our stomach tightens, our heart pounds, our hands shake, and our head feels like it's going to explode, we can't think clearly. We waste emotional energy. We may even unconsciously sabotage our own efforts. Self-control requires more than a plan. Over the long haul, it requires a calm nervous system.

Encourage your children to learn ways to relax. If they are consumed by anxiety, they will be unable to think clearly and keep their goals in sight. Many forms of meditation, yoga, and relaxation have been developed to reduce stress and to allow individuals to experience the calming effects of alpha brain-wave states. Regular physical exercise such as swimming or running reduces tension for many people. Similarly, various martial arts teach children ways to breathe, concentrate, and control their bodies—all critical to the development of self-control. While this chapter includes a number of activities successfully used to help children reduce stress, the field is a broad one. Parents should help their children explore as many options as possible by consulting books and investigating available classes. Relaxation is a highly personal matter; children should be encouraged to find those techniques that best suit *their* habits and temperament.

Ask your children to tell you what causes them stress. While sharing one's burdens with an empathetic listener can be calming in itself, the greatest value of this question is that it helps kids to identify the sources of their anxiety. Once children (and adults, for that matter) understand the situations or emotions that cause them the most concern, they can treat them as problems to be solved.

Relaxing is like any discipline—it is often easier to do with the support or presence of other people. Consider setting aside a time each day (it can be as short as fifteen minutes) when the whole family meditates or does yoga.

A PASSION AND A PLAN

You can have every resource to get somewhere, but without a destination, you're unlikely to leave home. It is the same with self-control. Sometimes self-control fails to emerge, not because *it* isn't there, but because *the goal* isn't there. For self-control to kick into gear, one needs a passion *and* a plan. In Chapter 11, we will discuss how parents who are nurturing can help to keep their children's passions alive. In this chapter, we look at ways to turn passions into identifiable goals.

Ask your children: "What would you do if you had a magic wand?" Some of their answers will be out of this world. But others—even the ones that sound most farfetched at first—are not impossible. Those are the ones to discuss. For example:

"I'd stop all the crime and the drugs and help homeless people find places to live." No, your child can't do it all by tomorrow, but she can articulate her own policy toward drugs. She can work in any number of ways to help the homeless. Help her to identify her options and perhaps she'll wish to get involved. A tremendous feeling of empowerment could result.

"I'd become a jet fighter pilot and an astronaut and go to Mars and . . ." If that is truly your child's ambition, you can help him see the connection between his goal and being more disciplined about his math homework. In the case of an older child, a summer job at a local airstrip (pay in the form of flying lessons), could be a wonderful and very real first step in the long flight to Mars.

The point of asking children this question is *not* to make them feel they must choose a career by age eleven, or that something is wrong with them if they don't have these types of goals. The point is to make them realize that whenever they're ready, there is such a thing as a magic wand. It's called self-control.

Ask your teenaged children how they would finish this sentence: "If I had more self-control, I would . . ." Go first yourself to break the ice and to be an example of honesty and humility. After everyone has had a chance to speak, talk about ways in which each person might be able to achieve his or her goal. In particular, see if you can think of ways that family members can help each other out: feedback about progress, reminders, encouragement, chart-keeping, etcetera. Use one another for moral support. The knowledge that someone else cares about your struggle (or is even just watching and noticing your efforts) can be a strong motivator.

Another good question to pose in the pursuit of self-control is: "What kind of person do I want to be?" If the preceding questions tend to unearth dreams and desired behavioral changes, this question tends to get at elements of character or personality: "I want to be nice, generous, funny, honest, daring, respected, and so on." Once children have identified desired attributes, talk about how close to attaining them they feel they are. Help children identify those situations in which they act the way they would like to, and those situations in which they don't. What provokes them to be "not the kind of person they want to be"? Once they recognize these situations, they can learn to avoid them or to develop strategies for handling them better. (Many of the activities at the end of this chapter will help them to do so.)

At times, our self-control is in concert with our desires. Mission and motivation overlap perfectly. At other times, the two are at cross purposes: What we really *want* is to go to the beach; what we *have to do* is write the term paper so we'll pass the course so we'll go to college so we'll . . . Much of the mastery of the self involves being able to act as one's own behavioral therapist. This is particularly true when we need to marshall our resources to get past low points and drudge work. While intrinsic satisfaction is a much-desired goal, let's face it, a lot of the things we have to do just aren't that much fun. One reward of having a plan is that one can plan to have a reward.

Encourage your children to think up treats and congratulations that they, or you, will provide at critical moments in recognition of successful self-control. Children can be notoriously hard on themselves. It's important for parents to show them how to be good to themselves.

A FOCUSED, FAITHFUL MIND

There are several things nurturing parents can do to help their child develop those powers of the mind that enhance self-control:

Encourage daydreaming. It is in the land of daydreams that goals are imagined, sights are set, and triumph is tried on for size. Daydreaming is not a frivolous pursuit that stands in the way of success. It is the foundation upon which achievement is built. Show your kids that you approve of daydreams. Share yours. Don't accuse them of doing nothing when they're staring at the ceiling or watching clouds go by. They're doing something very important—creating their future. As one boy we know said, "If you don't daydream you'll never get anywhere in life!"

Visualization is a form of directed daydreaming. It is a technique used extensively by athletes to place themselves in the circumstances of a game or competition: in their minds, they ski, serve, vault, kick, run, dive, and race. They rehearse success until they feel it, see it, taste it—and believe it will be theirs. This can be highly effective. In one study of two groups of high school basketball players, one group practiced free-throw shooting every day for a period of time while the other group simply *imagined* practicing free-throw shooting during that period. Afterward, both groups had improved their performance about the same!

Many of us use visualization without realizing it. When we rehearse a speech by mentally watching ourselves give it, or when we close our eyes and ski the slopes perfectly, we are visualizing. This mental projection of success is critical to self-control. In fact, one study found that inner-city kids are significantly poorer at visualization than suburban children. It was suggested that this may be one reason why dropout rates are so high in cities: students there are less able to imagine themselves as high school graduates—or as anything, for that matter. Without such a vision, what motivation is there for self-control?

Encourage your children to visualize themselves being successful. This is different from daydreaming in that it is more consciously directed. Children picture themselves being calm, capable, and triumphant. They see themselves scoring 100 on a test, swimming a race, walking to the stage at graduation, even winning the Nobel Prize! They can employ this strategy whenever they feel anxious, or their confidence lags. Obviously, visualization is not a substitute for studying, training, or hard work. However, the image of achievement created in the mind becomes real and helps to motivate children to exercise the self-control necessary to accomplish the task.

Often the difference between those who succeed and those who don't is that the former believed they could. Children need to have a vision of a compelling future if they are to engage their self-control. They need to trust themselves, and to have faith in their abilities.

It is easy for children to lose perspective when they encounter a minor setback during some task. Kids need to learn that every achievement has a history, and that failure and misadventure are part of it.

Nurturing parents can help their children to maintain focused and faithful minds in the face of obstacles or fears of failure:

Talk to your children about their minds. Help them to understand that the mind can be their most powerful ally or their most powerful enemy. Expectations can affect outcome. It is a choice they can make for themselves.

When your children are fixated on the "two steps backwards," remind them that they're still a step forward. Be careful that you don't discount their feelings; disappointment, sadness, frustration or embarrassment are all natural outcomes of a setback. But in the larger picture, in the history of their *ultimate* success, the lessons learned as a result of those temporary setbacks have truly brought them closer to their goal. Every time the Wright brothers crashed, for example, the dream of flight came one step nearer to reality.

Parents can teach their children to recognize when negative thinking threatens self-control. Conditioning techniques (some of which are described in this chapter's activities) can be used to strengthen mental focus. Nurtured children develop faith in their minds. This faith motivates high self-control. Much of reality is what we make of it. Much of what we make of it takes place in our minds. A child who gains control of his mind gains control of his world.

ACTIVITIES TO NURTURE SELF-CONTROL

NOW PLAYING ON YOUR NEIGHBORHOOD MIND!

Familiarize your children with the concept of visualization by asking them to imagine the first live elephant they ever saw. If they are successful in doing so, they should be able to see the wrinkles on the elephant's trunk! Have different family members propose items to visualize with which everyone is familiar: the family car, the refrigerator with its dozens of pictures and magnets, the leaky rowboat at the lake. Ask each other questions to test one's visualization skills. Write your name on your mind's blackboard; if it's really up there, you should be able to spell it backwards just by reading it. Try this with longer words.

KIM'S GAME

Materials: a piece of cloth 2-by-2-feet square, ten to twenty assorted small objects as described below, a flat area at least 2-by-2-feet square, pencils, paper.

Here's another good activity for sharpening children's visualization skills. Arrange the objects on the flat area in related groups of three or four. For example, place a grape, a plum, an apple, and a nut near each other. Any other types of small objects will do— sewing things; a bolt, a screw, and a nail; a spoon, a knife, and a fork.

Cover the objects before bringing the child or children in to observe them. Explain that this game was described by Rudyard Kipling in his book, *Kim,* which is about training young children to spy on the enemy during the revolution in India. When the group is settled, uncover the area for ten to thirty seconds (the amount of time depends on the age of the children—try it yourself first), then re-cover it. Ask the observers to write down each object they remember having seen. If everyone remembers them all, add some more objects and/or shorten the observation time.

Now retry the experiment with the same number of objects,

but use different ones *not* associated with each other. Almost certainly the children's success rate will fall. Explore why this occurred, and when they discover how helpful the association technique was to their ability to observe, ask them to suggest ways that they can use this technique in their daily lives.

If this activity is done in a group, no doubt some children will do better than others. Ask the more successful children to share what methods they used to do well with this task.

GET A GRIP ON YOURSELF!

As we mentioned earlier, a vital factor in controlling ourselves is being able to relax our tense body when we are under a great deal of stress. This is especially true when stress produces anger or rage. The following activity should be repeated many times. If your child makes it part of her daily routine, she will be able to use it even under extreme duress. Regular practice of this relaxation technique stretches and loosens the skeletal and muscular systems. The more relaxed the body is under normal circumstances, the longer it takes for stress to become debilitating.

Here are step-by-step instructions for practicing this activity with your child. You should use your own words when speaking with your child.

"We all lose control sometimes, often because we get angry or frustrated. We usually regret losing control. We feel bad, we get into trouble. We don't make the initial situation any better—sometimes it even becomes worse. Our lives are much happier when we can find ways to let go of our anger.

"Sometimes, however, we don't realize that anger or worry or fear is making us nervous. We're so filled up with the feeling, that we are unaware of our body's internal state. Can you think of some of the ways your body tells you that you are becoming angry or upset and need to relax?"

Help your child to identify these signals:

• You have a tightening in the stomach, or feel nauseous.
• You feel as though your head is going to explode.

- Your heart beats faster.
- Your hands may shake.
- Your body perspires.
- You may speak faster or much louder or softer than usual.
- Your voice and body may tremble.

"Everyone's reaction to anger is different. You have to learn what your warning signs are. When you see them coming on, take the following steps:

- Get away from the stressful situation, off by yourself. Often a good thing to do is go to the nearest restroom, or step outside for some air.
- Sit down and shake your hands and feet to loosen yourself up.
- Take a deep breath, hold it for ten seconds, and slowly let it out.
- Now take another breath and, holding it, bend your toes back toward your shins. Stay that way for ten seconds, then relax your feet as you let your breath out.
- Next, concentrate on your calves, tightening them while holding your breath, then relax and let the air out slowly.
- Repeat this process with your thighs, buttocks, abdomen, chest and shoulders, biceps and elbows, wrists and hands, neck and chin, and finally with your eyes and forehead.
- As a last step, take a deep breath, let it out, and think about what it means to feel completely at ease.

"Now try confronting what made you angry or anxious in the first place. You'll have a much better chance of discovering a good strategy for fixing the problem.

"If you do this every day (some people like to do it first thing in the morning, or just before going to sleep), you will get so good at it that you can use it instantly, even if others are around."

STOP THINKING THAT!

One of the greatest hindrances to self-management is fearful thinking about what *might* happen. This is known as *catastrophizing*.

There's nothing wrong with anticipating all the things that could go wrong if it prepares you to prevent possible dangers. Many of us, however, carry the process one step further. We go from thinking about the bad things that could happen to believing that those things *will* happen! These fears can paralyze us. When fear and negative thinking serve no purpose but to paralyze self-control, it's time for the "Stop Thinking That!" technique. This method can be taught to the individual child, but it works better if several of her friends participate in the practice session so they can reinforce each other later when the technique is needed. There are three steps to this method:

1.   First, have the entire group yell out the word "STOP" when you raise your hand. After a couple of tries, have the children close their eyes. This time they will yell the word "STOP" as soon as they hear some agreed-upon sound such as your ringing a bell or clapping your hands. Have them continue to do this, but after several more times, tell them to imagine a giant stop sign when they yell. After a couple of tries, have the children open their eyes. Now have the children yell the word "STOP" *silently* at some cue. Explain to them that this is the first step for them to take when they begin to think frightening thoughts that may cause them to lose control.

2.   The second step is to relax. Explain to the group that this will be a much shortened version of the relaxation technique described in the preceding activity. Have them close their eyes, take a deep breath, and hold it. Now have them breathe out slowly through their noses, letting their bodies relax and the tension flow out as they let the breath go. Ask them to try to feel a wave of relaxation moving from the top of their heads, to the face, shoulders, chest, and down all the way to their feet. Have them practice this a number of times, making sure they take deep breaths and let them out slowly.

Now have the children practice the first two steps together. When you raise your hand, they should yell "STOP" *silently* and then do the relaxation breathing. Make sure they separate the two parts and do not start the breathing exercise when they are still yelling "STOP."

3.   The third step involves imagining a pleasant experience.

Have the children close their eyes and imagine their favorite places. Remind them to listen for the sounds, smell the smells, and feel the air wherever they "go." Explain to them that traveling to their favorite place will help them relax and will distract them from whatever was making them lose control.

Now have the group practice all three steps together. Have them concentrate very hard on what they are doing and be careful not to overlap any of the parts. Remind them that this kind of control gives them an advantage over people who lose their control. Have them practice by imagining the last time they lost control and got angry or did something stupid that they now regret. This time, tell them to think about how they could have avoided the bad experience by using the three-step "Stop Thinking That!" method.

CREATE YOUR OWN WORLD

Materials: an old kickball or beach ball, or materials to make one out of papier-mâché (a balloon, newspapers, flour-and-water paste); a bounty of construction materials: paper tubes, tin foil, bottle caps, small boxes, ribbons, Popsicle sticks, twigs, fabric, etcetera.), markers, and rubber cement.

Read your child *The Little Prince* by Antoine de Saint-Exupéry. In this story a child is in charge of his own planet. Now have your child imagine what *his* planet might look like. Ask questions that help him to visualize what's there. Once he has a clear image in his mind, suggest that he build it, using the beach ball as a base. Encourage him to be detailed as well as visionary. He might also want to make another planet to inhabit with his best friend, or planets with special purposes, such as a school planet or an amusement-park planet.

OTHER ACTIVITIES

• Often it is easier to control ourselves when we can understand the feelings and motivations of the person with whom we are interacting. This activity can be done anytime—commuting to school, waiting in line, or while eating dinner. Ask your child to describe the present situation from the point of view of someone/ something else. Say to your child, for example, "If the headlight of the car could talk, what would it say right now?" Ask her to narrate the trip from the point of view of the rearview mirror or from the perspective of the steering wheel or the blinking yellow light at the next intersection. What might a conversation between the stop sign and the car's windshield wiper be like?

This activity can also be practiced in response to human inter- actions that you and your child observe: "What do you think the grocery cart would say to the little boy whose mother just scolded him?" "If that girl had a conversation with the man who just butted into line, what do you think they would say?"

• Empathy is crucial to self-control because an understanding of the feelings of others can provide strong motivation to stick to a plan or alter one's behavior. Here's another activity designed to help children develop empathy. They do this by looking at the world from various unique perspectives. The best way to intro- duce this game is to model what your child will do. First, glue a picture of your child to the top of a stick. (A paint stirrer is perfect for this.) Next, hide the stick someplace in a room and ask your child to find his picture but not to remove it from the spot. When he finds it, go over to the spot and start to tell a story. For example, if the stick-picture was hidden in between the leaves of a large plant, you might start by saying, "Here I am in the jungle! The ground is very wet and soft. The birds . . ." Once your child has the idea, have him finish the story.

Hide the stick again, and let him create the next story from the start. (Be sure to locate the picture in places that are rich in stimuli for a good story.) Help your child along at the start of a story by asking questions that build on what he has said.

Several children can play by hiding each other's stick-pictures and then telling stories to the group.

11

HEAD OVER HEELS
ABOUT EVERYTHING:
PASSION

*T*he children we studied were passionate—inflamed with ideas, vehement in feeling, lustful for life.

"I don't know why," said one parent, "but I feel like I'm often defending my child's intensity. I get the impression that society doesn't care for it much, except maybe in romance novels. But I'll tell you, what really scares me isn't kids with passion, it's kids without any. In my work as a school counselor, I see kids every day who simply don't care about anything. Those are the ones I worry about."

Another concurred. "I think this relates to something that came up recently in my family. My son, who just turned seventeen, announced that he doesn't want to go to college. I've always believed that college isn't for everyone—at least as far as other people's kids are concerned. For my kid, of course, it was never a question. Well, what my son wants to do as soon as he graduates from high school is move to L.A. and pursue his music. It's not a whim, he's been playing and writing music since he was five, and I know he's good. All through high school his band had more jobs than they knew what to do with. A few months ago somebody heard them and wants to help them produce a demo tape. So what do we do? I know the odds. Do we put them ahead of my kid's dream? I'd be a hypocrite to everything I've tried to teach my son if I did that. We talked about this for weeks and we decided we're not going to stand in the way. And if he makes it big, well, my wife and I will retire and my son can support us in grand style!"

It's not easy when children want to strike out on roads less traveled. Passion has certainly led many kids and adults astray. But what the kids of nurturing parents have going for them is the fact that their passion runs side by side with their good judgment, responsibility, and willingness to delay gratification.

"When I was growing up," said one father, "the worst thing you could do was show that you were head over heels about anything. It wasn't until college that I found people who admitted to being smitten. It's always been a source of pleasure to me that my kids seem to care so deeply about so many things."

"Like what?" we asked.

"Like reading. Collecting. Photography. Saving the world. Recycling. Acid rain. Last year my eldest ran a fund drive at school for the homeless. This year all three of them staggered around the house gasping 'secondhand smoke,' choking and dying until I gave up smoking. My wife was thrilled."

As we learned more about these children, we were continually struck by the intensity and range of their enthusiasms, and the depth and duration of their feelings. Their personalities encompassed all of *Roget's* synonyms for the word *passionate*: ardent, eager, devoted, keen, zestful, fascinated. But "passionate" has other shadings as well: hotheaded, fiery, infatuated, obsessed, agitated. How do you keep passion from becoming a destructive force—full of sound and fury but signifying nothing? We put these questions to the parents in our study.

One parent expressed an observation shared by many: "Nobody could be more passionate than my son—about his friends, his plans, his interests. But he also has a system of checks and balances. He's passionate, but he's responsible. If his head is in the clouds, his feet are still on the ground—maybe on tiptoes, but at least they're touching!"

A child's passion, like a river, must have boundaries if it is to flow with vigor and direction. The system of checks and balances referred to by this parent provides these boundaries. Within the family, they take the form of clear values, parental role-modeling, and good communication. Within the child, they take the form of empathy, integrity, and good judgment.

"Ah, but if passion responds to reason," one might ask, "is it really passion?" Yes. When passion fails to respond to reason, it is obsession. The child (or adult) who is obsessed is driven beyond passion. He is possessed by it, rather than in control of it. To be

passionate about an activity or pursuit demands a level of awareness that allows the person to own it, and to understand why he
cares about it so much. People who are obsessed are usually
unable to offer any explanations or justifications for their driven
behavior.

There are a number of things parents can do to encourage passion
in their children:

• Ask your child to explain what it is that makes her love doing
something to the point that nothing else seems to matter. The
purpose in this is not to take the magic out of her activity, but
rather to help her identify what she loves about it. This explicit
awareness often allows a child to make connections to new and
related interests.

• Let children burn the midnight oil. Allow the muses to take
kids outside of ordinary schedules and routines. It can be a lot
healthier for a child to chase a creative thought than to get an
extra hour's sleep.

• Be spontaneous. Let the spirits move you. Rush off to a movie.
Dash downtown to a Chinese restaurant. Gather the clan and say,
"Hey, does anyone besides me feel like doing something *different*
this afternoon?"

• Expose children to the delights of the sensual world: bub-
blebaths, swimming in a mountain stream, watching the sunset.
Take them to a sauna, a daring art exhibit, an avant garde concert.
Sometimes passion needs a spark to be ignited—provide children
with opportunities to see, hear, touch, taste, and smell. Let them
snuggle frosty-nosed into a sleeping bag under a trillion stars, let
them stand under a warm April shower or dive into a dusty leaf
pile. These can be passionate experiences for young children.
Think how many of your own childhood memories are sensual
ones—a roaring bonfire spitting orange confetti into the night sky,
a moonlit ocean speaking in silver-tipped tongues.

Many people see child-raising as a process of pruning. Here a
snip, there a snip—and soon the child will be growing in the
desired shape. Nurturing parents see child-raising as a process of
providing good soil, water, and plenty of sunlight. Every time a

parent says, "Calm down," "Don't get so excited," "You're being silly," or "Don't you ever know when to stop?", they snip away at their child's emotional energy. To be fair to our horticultural analogy, sometimes pruning is a necessary step in floral self-actualization. Nurturing parents, however, do this cautiously. They think twice before saying anything that puts a damper on their children's emotional expression.

Emotions atrophy if they are suppressed. Boys who are told never to cry may lose the ability to feel sad. Girls who are enjoined against feeling anger may lose the ability to get mad. Children who are never loved are unable to love. Not surprisingly, many psychologists and law-enforcement officials see gang violence as the result of the loveless conditions in which so many inner-city children are raised. It is difficult to learn to value life, respect property, and care about others if one grows up in an environment of poverty and neglect.

Nurturing parents allow children the full range of their feelings. The pruning of emotional expression that does occur is usually done by the children themselves, as their empathy and sense of responsibility grow. While not all passion leads to greatness, surely most greatness arises out of passion. We do not know if the children in our study will grow up to do great things. We are confident, however, that almost all of them will grow up to lead great lives.

ACTIVITIES TO NURTURE PASSION

THE CASE OF THE SCHOOLYARD JUNK

Suggest that your child and some friends become "schoolyard detectives." The goal of this activity is to determine who is most responsible for littering the schoolyard, and to do something about it. It encourages the development of passionate feelings, in this case about the "grubbiness" of the place where they play.

The first question the detective must answer is, "Who are the major culprits?" To find out, the team will need to make a reconnaissance of the schoolyard and collect a representative sample of litter. The litter should be sorted into types, and the types sorted according to the likely age, gender, etcetera, of those responsible. For example, it could be deduced that cigarette butts are probably from older persons, candy wrappers are from children, and soda cans are from the machine at the gas station. The detectives may need to keep the schoolyard under surveillance to confirm their suspicions.

Once the group has decided who's responsible, they should organize a campaign to get the culprits to change their behavior. (Teachers who have tried this activity tell us that in many cases they find that "the enemy is them"!) There are many things that could be done. Designing and hanging posters, and getting a spot on the local radio station are two examples. Hopefully, this will be the beginning of a long-lasting and passionate concern for the environment.

Extensions:

Have the detectives target other sites for investigation: a nearby park or nature trail, a rural lane, a city street.

Encourage the group to pursue other causes they are passionate about. Many children feel strongly about animal rights, gun control, pollution, nuclear disarmament, helping the poor and the homeless, or racial and sexual discrimination. It's important for kids to feel that they *can* make a difference. Let them join organizations, pay dues, give to charity, and volunteer their time.

As a family, commit yourselves to a cause. Sponsor a foster child overseas. Make a tangible sacrifice and translate it into a donation to those who are less fortunate. March for hunger! Protest at the State House!

DON'T BE A WET BLANKET

This activity is not to be done with children, but rather by yourself and, if you like, with your spouse. It will help you avoid accidentally pouring cold water on your child's budding passionate interests. The first step is to think about the things that you care about passionately, and the times that you have felt passionately involved with an activity or another person. Go all the way back to your youth and childhood—visualize those moments, recall the sensations that accompanied them. This sensitization will make you more ready to recognize passion in your own children.

The second step is to translate that sensitivity into your interactions with your child. Putting on a fresh lens with which to view the sometimes puzzling or "cute" pursuits of your child will nurture the trait of passion in both you and him. For example, if your child seems engrossed in acquiring and wearing clothing that you consider unsightly, don't hurry into an argument. Instead, ask him to explain the "look." Realize that his actions may well be an expression of passion—passion for a style, passion for belonging with peers, passion for self-expression through his dress.

Similarly, try to take your child's first "puppy love" seriously. There is often a strong temptation to view this early approach to love as humorous. Recall your own first venture toward a relationship—you'll probably realize that it was the farthest thing from funny at the time.

By analyzing your own passionate feelings, you will best be able to achieve empathy with those of your child.

OTHER ACTIVITIES

• In Louise Fitzhugh's delightful book, *Harriet the Spy*, Harriet keeps a detailed notebook of observations, musings, and speculations about favorite people, places, and ideas. In the story, Harriet not only records *real* observations, she records imaginary conversations as well. She becomes extremely excited by these imaginings.

Try reading this book to your child. Then encourage her to become a "spy" in her own house/town/school and to record her observations and speculations in a private journal. You may have to explain to perplexed others what all the writing is about, but let your child pursue her journal passionately. Protect and nurture the spirit of adventure that such immersion in a personal project can bring!

• Children are natural collectors. Help your child think about something(s) he would love to collect. Encourage him to expand his collection thoughtfully, and respect his pursuit by helping him find space for storage and display.

• Who are your heroes? Pick one or two famous people you have admired, and obtain a biography of them. Read these stories with or to your child, and explain why you feel your heroes were (are) so extraordinary. Select biographies of individuals who you think might appeal to your child. Encourage her to learn as much as she can about people who led great and fascinating lives.

• Discuss with your child the meaning of the word *passion*. Consider the motivations for and the boundaries around passionate feelings.

• Engage your child and some of his friends in a discussion of the difference between an obsession and a passion.

• Being passionate usually involves having a strong sense of purpose. What are your reasons for living? What are things you would die for? Deep philosophical discussions fan the flames of passion.

• If your child feels strongly about an issue, encourage her to write a letter about it. She could send it to a public official or corporate executive, or to the editor of her local or school newspaper.

• Guide obsessions into passions by provoking your child's creativity. Turn passivity into productivity. If your child watches rock videos for hours on end, suggest that he produce one himself. (A neighborhood band might be thrilled to be the stars.) If your child sits glued to the television set, suggest that he write a screenplay for his favorite show. If he devours comic books, suggest that he invent his own.

• One of the joys of having a passion is finding others who share it. Often this happens naturally, particularly when the interest is common to many children: sports, cars, music, skateboarding, computer games, and so on. Sometimes, though, a child's interest may be quite singular. Perhaps there just aren't many other kids in the neighborhood who are mad about designing houses, playing bagpipes, or perfecting a cheese soufflé. Somewhere, however, there are. Help your child to find them. Practically every interest or hobby has a newsletter, magazine, or national organization associated with it. Post notices on computer bulletin boards. Place an ad in a relevant publication. Write a letter requesting penpals. Sometimes expanding the search to people beyond your child's age will do the trick—there may be students at a nearby college, retirees, or adults employed in the field who would enjoy being a mentor to a younger enthusiast.

12

GOING TO YOUR HIGH SCHOOL CLASS REUNION:
TOLERANCE OF AMBIGUITY

"*O*f course I want to do the right thing!" said a teenager of our acquaintance. "I'm just not sure what that is. I just can't make up my mind!" It is hard to know what to do in an ambiguous situation because the relevant facts are missing, the rules are unclear, or the right procedures are unavailable. (Sounds a lot like life!) For a five-year-old, the first day of kindergarten would be an example of an unclear situation, for a forty-three-year-old, it might be a high school class reunion.

People react differently to ambiguous situations. A situation that causes mild concern in some may cause a desire to flee in others. The ability to remain open-minded in the face of ambiguity (and sometimes to really enjoy it) is a hallmark of the creative children we studied. As Jacob Getzels of the University of Chicago puts it, "The core of creativity is not in withdrawal from the world, it is in openness to the world." What the average person finds distressing, the creative person finds intriguing. What the average person finds threatening, the creative person finds exciting. This higher tolerance of ambiguity fosters the ability to react creatively. In essence, creative people, people with high tolerance of ambiguity, are willing to take risks.

To children, the whole world is ambiguous. Picture an infant responding to faces, expressions, sounds, and motions. Picture a first grader meeting new authority figures, new expectations for behavior, and new intellectual concepts. Picture a young adolescent confronting puberty, academic demands, and social pressures. How children react to the unfamiliar indicates how well they tolerate ambiguity. And the more they tolerate ambiguity, the more they will enjoy life.

In many ways, child-raising can be described as the process by which parents shape their children's attitudes toward the strange and the unknown. This process inevitably reflects their own tolerance of ambiguity. Parents who face life with distrust and fear will be hard-pressed not to pass this attitude on to their children. Similarly, parents who embrace life with confidence and enthusiasm will be presenting a positive model for their children to assimilate. Parents who were taught to have a low tolerance of ambiguity can still encourage their kids to higher levels, but it takes a good deal of self-awareness to break the cycle.

The best way to measure your child's tolerance of ambiguity is by observing how he or she reacts to new situations. How does your infant respond to strangers, to new playmates, to unfamiliar environments, to unexpected noises or physical sensations?

How does your elementary school-age child respond to the procession of "first-time" events that march through his or her life—new teachers, subjects and work expectations, new social configurations of cooperation and competition, new opportunities to acquire skills and display competency?

How does your older child respond to the ambiguity of adolescence: Who am I? Where am I going? What do I value? There are few rules to guide the transition between childhood and adulthood; adolescents travel virgin territory when coming to grips with feelings involving sexuality, self-worth, societal expectations, and peer relationships. The love-hate relationship they may have with you, their parents, is yet another example of stability turned topsy-turvy.

Adolescents with low tolerance of ambiguity may take their failures as signs of worthlessness; they may feel the world is out to get them; they may mask their fears with drugs or withdrawal; they may seek the low profile of rigid conformity to rules.

Those adolescents with high tolerance of ambiguity assume responsibility for themselves and believe that their actions matter; they make their own decisions and can be flexible about them: they are sensitive to their own feelings and those of others; they see setbacks as puzzles to solve.

The essence of tolerance of ambiguity is being able to take risks. The unknown is a scary thing. People who are different from us may seem dangerous or make us feel uncomfortable. Many people rush to foreclose options just to maintain sameness in their lives. This stands in the way of growth. The children in our study have high tolerance of ambiguity. They rush out to greet life, not because they are fearless, but because they have learned to deal with fear. With their parents' support, they were encouraged to take reasonable risks as they grew.

We should point out that none of the parents in our study spoke of "tolerance of ambiguity" in describing their children. What they spoke of was their children's ability to take risks and to handle fear. For the rest of this chapter, we will speak of it primarily in those terms as well.

One of the hardest things for parents to do is determine what constitutes an appropriate level of risk-taking. The following example shows the type of judgment parents have to exercise daily.

When the daughter of one of the parents in our study was four years old, she proudly displayed to her father the first letter she had ever written to Grandma. "I want to mail it myself," she proclaimed. But the trip to the mailbox, several blocks away, involved crossing two streets. As he rummaged in his desk for a stamp, this father grappled with the dilemma that all parents face—how to encourage his child's independence without exposing her to undue risk.

He concluded that the dangers of the walk, when viewed against the importance of supporting his daughter's initiative, were small. After rehearsing the route and reviewing safety rules, he sent the four-year-old on her confident way. Fortunately, none of the neighbors called the police to report the strange man, darting behind the bushes and trees, who appeared to be stalking a little girl carrying a letter to the mailbox!

When is risk-taking valuable to the development of tolerance of ambiguity? And when is it just downright dangerous? All parents wrestle with these questions as they watch their children teeter on the top of a jungle gym, career around a skateboard ramp, or participate in the rites of peer culture. Risks, however, are necessary to growth, and children who are risk-takers will build self-confidence, overcome fear, and expand their knowledge and skills. All the world's a stage for these kids' feats of derring do.

("Daddy, watch me!") They want to climb the highest, swim the farthest, and ride the fastest. Unable to resist a challenge, they sometimes push the limits of acceptable social behavior, taunting friends and making wisecracks to adults. Once experience rubs the self-destructive edges off their behavior, however, these kids, in their willingness to take more moderate risks, will have a valuable asset.

What is a healthy level of risk-taking? Imagine yourself playing a game of ring toss. In this game, the farther you are from the pin, the more points you score for a successful toss. The first pin gets a score of 1, the tenth a score of 10. You get ten throws. At which pin would you most likely aim?

This game illustrates the continuum of "risk-taking." People who aim at the number one position take a very limited risk, but a ringer is only worth 1 point. Even if they ring the pin all ten times, their maximum possible score is only 10. Those who aim at the tenth pin have only one-tenth the likelihood of scoring; even though the tenth pin is worth 10, their most likely score is also 10 (1 success $\times$ 10 points). Those willing to take a moderate risk would probably aim at the fifth pin. Here the likely score would be 25 (5 successes $\times$ 5 points).

While these figures obviously only hold for this particular game, they probably reflect the odds of the real world. Children who take either tiny risks or huge risks are less likely to be successful than those who take moderate risks. The child who is socially timid may have just as few friends as the child who is socially reckless. The child who approaches others with a mix of confidence and caution, however, will be most likely to find rewarding personal relationships.

What determines a child's risk-taking capacity? To a certain degree, genes. Some kids pop hell-bent into the world, clamoring for experience, eager to leap into the unknown. They explore and expand, and when disaster strikes, they may be dazed but rarely daunted. Other kids are more cautious by nature. Hesitant to venture into unfamiliar territory, they want to preview the script before taking the part.

While temperament plays its role, ultimately, a child's tolerance of ambiguity is most strongly determined by the consequences which ensue from taking risks. Positive consequences can encourage timid children to take more risks. Negative consequences can teach reckless children to look more carefully before leaping. Negative consequences, however, can also dishearten moderate risk-takers over time. This is why it is so important for parents to support their children through inevitable periods of failure or rejection. Much of this chapter will explain how this can be done.

Not all consequences can be predicted. This, of course, triggers the dilemma parents face as they agonize over decisions to limit and/or expand their children's freedom. Authoritarian parents deal with this problem by placing their children on a short leash. Rather than equip their kids with the skills necessary to navigate in the world, they seek to limit the world. They build their trust, not in their child, but in their ability to control their child's life:

> "No, your friend cannot drive you to school." (One less chance to get in an accident.)
> "No, you cannot go on a date." (One less chance to get pregnant or to impregnate.)
> "No, you cannot go on the school ski trip." (One less chance to break a leg or to drink or use drugs.)

It is a fallacy to believe that these prohibitions reduce a child's risk of accident, pregnancy, or drug use. The tragedy of this approach is that it can cripple a child's development, or force her to adopt a secret and deceptive life, destroying the parent-child relationship.

Permissive parents deal with their children's risk-taking by ignoring it. They close their eyes to their kids' behavior, be it wildly uncontrolled or fearfully withdrawn.

By their nature, authoritative parents can set the stage for parent-child conflicts over risk-taking. By allowing their children some freedoms, authoritative parents indirectly spotlight those they deny. Since the perception of risk is in the eye of the beholder, children of authoritative parents often find it difficult to see why they're permitted to do some things but not others. Thus, conflict can occur in these homes as youngsters fight to maintain and expand their freedom.

Nurturing parents view risk-taking as a prerequisite to growth.

They *want* their children to take appropriate risks, and the attitudes and values of the home encourage it:

- Such parents trust their children's reliability and good judgment.
- Good communication ensures that options and outcomes can be discussed.
- Children know that the ultimate decision is theirs to make, so they don't need to be rebellious.
- Positive self-image means that children won't take crazy risks just to prove something to themselves or others.
- Positive self-image means that children will take reasonable risks because they know they can handle the failure or rejection that may result.

One of the major stumbling blocks to achieving these goals, however, is that children and adults see risks differently. For example:

A parent is trying to decide whether to let her fourteen-year-old son go with some friends to see a midnight movie at a theater in a nearby town. Apart from the late hour, this mother's major concern is that the driver of the expedition will be a newly-decorated-with-a-license sixteen-year-old. Meanwhile, her son sees the risks of the evening in a different context: the ramifications of various combinations of contact between his right arm and the girl he intends to sit next to.

"The thing I find hardest about being a parent," one mother in our study observed, "is letting my child take risks. Intellectually, I know it's necessary. But I'm not going to pretend it's easy. It's hard for me to accept the fact that no matter how careful I am, the cosmic wheel of fortune is always spinning."

Said another mother: "Every time I hear of something terrible happening to a child, I add it to this ever-expanding list of prohibitions I keep in my head: no ice-skating except at the rink, no wrestling, no snowmobiles, no motor scooters, no jet-skis, no speedboats. I know it's ridiculous—you lock your child up in his room thinking he's safe, and an airplane could fall on the house.

You don't let him wrestle, and, God forbid, he'll break his neck falling out of bed. I know there's only so much you can do to keep kids safe, but as a parent, it never seems enough."

"When our first child was born," added a father, "I remember how my wife and I used to watch him sleep. There was something absolutely primal about it—the sense of responsibility, the instinct to protect. The feelings were incredible. But there was also this breathtaking feeling of vulnerability—if anything ever happened to him, I'd never be able to forgive myself. I think that's one reason parents say no to their kids. It's not to protect the kids so much as to protect the parents. At least that way, if the kid goes ahead and gets hurt, it isn't the parents' fault."

HELPING LOW-RISK TAKERS TO TAKE MORE RISKS

The macho American culture does little to help children recognize fear as a natural and even healthy response to the new and the unknown. Many children who are afraid to take risks have never learned to understand and deal with their fears. It is _fear of fear_ that keeps them frozen. There are a number of things parents can do to encourage fearful children to undertake more challenges:

Talk with your children about fear. Older children can understand the evolutionary role of fear in ensuring human survival. Younger children can learn that everybody is afraid of different things. Being brave doesn't mean that you don't have fears; it means that you move forward in spite of them. If children learn to accept their fears rather than feel ashamed of them, they can then direct their emotional energy toward overcoming fearfulness.

Acknowledge your own fears, past and present. Remember that from a child's point of view most parents appear to have been super-children who, if they didn't trudge twelve miles to school through ten feet of snow (like _their_ parents), at least ticked off the milestones of childhood with fearless aplomb. It is much healthier for children to know that parents had (and have) fears, than it is for them to mythologize parents as being fearless.

Help your child to identify his fears. The direct question, "What are you afraid of?" is generally not the best way to do this. For one thing, your child may not know what frightens him, in which case he now feels ignorant as well as fearful. For another thing, this question puts kids on the defensive. It implies that there is something wrong with having fears.

Better to approach the issue indirectly. If your child balks at an activity (a school trip, gym class, going to a sleep-over), ask him to describe or imagine the experience: "What do you think it will be like? What was it like last time? What was the worst part about it? What was the best part? How would you make it different this time? Do you think Teddy the Bear would want to go? What do you think Teddy is afraid might happen?" It is often easier for children to verbalize "Teddy's" fears than their own. They can tell you that Teddy hates to take showers in gym, or that Teddy thinks the teacher is mean and stupid because she makes kids stand in front of the class as punishment. By listening carefully, parents can find clues to their children's fears.

If your child is reluctant to do something, ask her, "What's the worst thing that could happen?" Her answer might be, "They might laugh at me." "It wouldn't work." "I'd lose." "Everybody'd think I was dumb." Consequences often become less dire when they can be imagined. Once children begin to realize that they will survive "the worst thing," they are more willing to take risks.

Let your child know that his willingness to take risks says far more about his character than what happens afterward. This shouldn't imply that consequences are unimportant. The point is for children to take pride in their efforts—that they entered the competition, issued the invitation, attempted the journey—these are the things that really count. Your child should keep this in mind as he nurses his disappointments.

Walk your child in advance through anxiety-producing events. If this can be done in actual fact, so much the better. For example, if your daughter fears riding on a bus, let her take the initiative by depositing the money, pulling the cord, asking the driver for assistance. Explain what you are going to see, point out familiar landmarks, and ask questions so that your child will narrate her expectations and recognize her mastery of the situation. "What would you do if . . . ?" "What would you tell 'Teddy' to do if he misses the stop?"

And finally, don't ever say "I told you so": "I told you there was nothing to be afraid of"; "I told you it wouldn't be so scary." By diminishing the scariness, you diminish the accomplishment. Focus on the fact that your child overcame his fear: "Even though you were afraid, you went right ahead and did it! You must feel very proud of yourself."

It is important that parents not minimize or belittle their children's fears or imagined consequences. Any adult who is afraid of dogs, flying, or giving speeches knows that fear and risk perception are entirely personal matters. Being told that "there's nothing to be afraid of," or that "flying is the safest form of travel" doesn't do one bit of good. As adults, we tend to forget how threatening the world can seem to children: schoolyard bullies, snarling dogs, endless evaluation and opportunity to fail. Children take risks every time they raise their hands in class, step up to the plate, venture a conversation, whisper a confidence.

Often, all children want is for their parents to know that life is hard. It's a bit like the toddler who has to show Daddy his bruise in order to forget about it. Parents can help timid children by acknowledging the pain, embarrassment or confusion their children feel. Pretending that feelings aren't there won't make them go away. The important message for parents to communicate is not that their child "shouldn't be afraid," but that however bad things get, they know their child can handle it. "You must be so disappointed. . . . It must have been so difficult. . . . That must have hurt so much. . . . But look how you kept going. . . . I'm so proud of the way you tried again. . . . Remember how beautifully you managed when that happened once before?" This way, children build confidence in their ability to deal with fears and consequences.

HELPING HIGH-RISK TAKERS TO BECOME MORE MODERATE

Most children will want to climb up on the radiator until they learn for themselves what "Hot!" means. Children need to experience their mistakes. Nothing teaches faster than error. This isn't to suggest, however, that parents stand by while their children swim toward disaster. Sometimes, a time-out in all the excitement is enough to get kids to see where their actions are heading and to make necessary changes in course. Parents can provide this pause by asking questions or offering suggestions: "Do you think that adding a brick might make it a bit more sturdy?" "How do you think your friend will feel if you do that?" "Maybe it would be easier if you waited until the ground were dry." If children insist on doing it their own way, let them. That's how they learn. If they are forced to do it your way, all they've learned is that adults have more power than kids.

Don't shield your children from the consequences of their actions (so long as the actions do not endanger themselves or others). If you're going to allow kids to make mistakes, it's only fair that you also allow them to experience the consequences. Avoid the temptation to rush in and sweep up the mess. It is when kids have to repair and replace, apologize and admit, squirm and blush, that they will think twice the next time. Allow children this dignity, the more so by being sympathetic and supportive as they face the music: "I know how much you looked forward to going." "It must feel terrible to have to save your money all over again."

Sometimes, of course, you will have to step in—to wash a skinned knee or talk to school officials, for example. Helping children with the resources available to adults, however, is quite different from insulating them from the consequences of their actions. Even when you go to bat for your child, many consequences remain that are the child's alone to face: a curtailed social calendar, the loss of a good friendship, a course to be repeated in summer school.

Shower high-risk takers with attention and affection at times when they are calm and engaged in low- or no-risk activities. This will help to discourage any high-risk behavior motivated by a desire for attention.

Children who engage in high-risk behavior may not see it as such: "Everybody else does it"; "I'm not going to get hurt"; "Nobody'll mind." Where a difference in perception exists, let your children know exactly what you're afraid might happen. (This can be a valuable exercise for parents, too.) Present your concerns as an issue of *your feelings* as opposed to *your child's behavior*: "I worry that you're going to get hurt," is quite different from, "*You're* going to hurt yourself." The former focuses on the parent's worry, while the latter casts a slur upon the child's capabilities. If a child doesn't feel pressured to defend his competence, he will be more likely to consider the effects of his actions on parental feelings, and to modify behavior accordingly. Most children will not mind calling home if it will help Mom and Dad with their "worrying problem." They will resent it, however, if it is due to a clear lack of trust.

Don't be afraid to be the bad guys. Sometimes kids need (and want) to be saved from themselves. They get in over their heads with their peers or with their fantasies. At these times, what they want more than anything is to be able to say, "My parents won't let me." Nurturing parents are never afraid to step in when they see the possibility of injury or permanent harm occurring to their child or others, or when the price paid for a lesson learned is simply too high. Such times are rare, however, since nurtured kids usually come quite readily to mature and responsible perspectives.

Where high-risk activity persists in the face of repeated negative consequences, professional help may be advisable to identify the causes of such self-destructive behavior. Anger, fear, depression, or even neurological damage may be motivating the child to hurt herself or others.

Parents need to be wary of projecting their own current or past fears onto their kids. If, as children themselves, they were afraid of contact sports, spending the night away from home, or dating, they might now, as adults, have a desire to protect their children from the risks they sought to avoid while growing up. Similarly, parents' current fears—of meeting new people, camping in the wilderness, or getting lost in a big city—could lead them to invest their children's activities with far greater risk than truly exists.

The opposite can happen as well. Motivated by the desire that their own children should not be so constrained by fears as they themselves were, some parents may push their kids into activities and experiences for which they are not ready and which do not interest them. Most of these pitfalls can be avoided. When looking at risk-related issues of child-raising, parents can ask themselves:

- How did I feel about taking risks as a child? What did I do?
- Am I nursing any risk-related childhood wounds?
- What were my parents' attitudes toward risk-taking?
- How do I feel about participating in these types of activities today?
- Am I a low-, moderate-, or high-risk taker?
- Could I be projecting my feelings onto my child?
- Could my child be modeling my own attitudes?

When confronting a specific situation, reality checking can best be done by completing one of these sentences:

I *don't want* my child to do such and such because_____.
I *want* my child to do such and such because_____.

When forced to specify their fears or motivations, many parents come to realize that their worries may have little to do with the actual risks involved. The real fear is sometimes of a different, less obvious nature:

- a fear of losing their child's love;
- a fear of their child's increasing independence;
- a fear of aging—symbolized by their child's growing maturity.

Parents can search for hidden agendas in their feelings and attitudes by comparing the limits they set with those of other parents. While the actions of others are sometimes most valuable as indications of what *not* to do ("I don't care if Julie's mother lets her stay out all night, the answer is still no!"), they can provide parents with useful comparisons for decision-making.

As parents help their children learn to assess and take healthy risks, they can take comfort in the fact that generally kids do not like paying for items they accidentally destroy. They do not wish to look foolish, stupid, uncool, ill-advised, or otherwise out of control of the events upon which their reputations hinge. They do not want to prove their parents right and themselves wrong.

When one thinks of risks and children, one tends to think first of physical or external things—cars, bikes, jungle gyms, injuries. In that accidents are the greatest threat to a child's life (they are the number one killer of adolescents), this makes perfect sense. One also thinks of issues of independence: at what age is it appropriate for a child to walk in the neighborhood by himself, to take a bus alone, to ride her bike to a friend's house, to date the opposite sex? From the child's point of view, however, EVERYTHING can seem like a risk: stating an opinion, asking a question, volunteering an answer, learning a new skill, expressing a feeling, *feeling* a feeling. And no wonder, for if we come back to the definition of ambiguity with which we began this chapter— a situation in which relevant facts are missing, rules are unclear, or the right procedures are unavailable—we realize that children face ambiguity every day of their lives. They take risks every day of their lives.

If ambiguity rocks the child's boat, however, good self-esteem steadies it. Kids who feel confident and secure are better able to face uncertainty than kids who fearfully look outside of themselves for approval and direction. When parents bolster their child's self-esteem, they strengthen their child's tolerance of ambiguity. And heightened tolerance of ambiguity in turn raises self-esteem. It is in this cyclical climate of nourishment that the integrated personality traits of the well-nurtured child are most likely to grow.

ACTIVITIES TO NURTURE TOLERANCE OF AMBIGUITY

• Suggest to your child that he create his own "daredevil course" to navigate on bike, wagon, skateboard, or even, in winter, sled or skis. The key is to help him to set the proper level of risk so that the course is challenging without being dangerous. He may want to construct ramps, jumps, and tunnels, and to set up obstacles or targets. Encourage him to think in terms of factors such as balance, speed, accuracy, and distance. Be sure he thinks about safety precautions such as clothing and protective gear, "landing" spots (sand or grass as opposed to concrete), and hazards to avoid such as rocks or posts. This activity is excellent for helping children to understand and determine appropriate levels of risk-taking.

• Camping and wilderness survival are two terrific ways to develop a child's tolerance of ambiguity, but these activities require long-term preparation as children learn the skills involved. If parents are unable to teach them, children can learn such skills from books, scouting, summer camp, and Outward Bound programs.

Young children can begin by camping out on the porch, or sleeping in a pup tent in the backyard. This presents considerable ambiguity as they face new sounds, night shadows, and spooky feelings. For older children with the proper training, the challenge can be extended by letting them spend a night or weekend in the wilderness where they will need to deal with unknown conditions and match wits with the environment. This activity can be done both as a solo experience in which being alone creates much of the ambiguity, or as a group experience in which the newness comes from being with friends in different and more intense circumstances.

• Give your child a pencil and a sheet of paper with random dots all over it. Do not number the dots. Ask your child to connect the dots in any way she likes to make a picture. Once she gets used to the idea, she may enjoy making up her own dots to connect.

• Make your own jigsaw puzzles by pasting duplicate family photographs or pictures from magazines on cardboard and then cutting them up. Have your child assemble the pieces, but don't say what the finished puzzle is supposed to look like. See if your child can tolerate the uncertainty and figure it out.

• Present your child with three to twelve photographs or pictures cut from magazines or newspapers. Ask him to tell you a story which incorporates every picture and/or character.

• Hand your child a sheet of paper with a column of symbols on it that you have drawn. These can be recognized symbols (an addition sign, a one-way arrow, gender symbols, skull and crossbones), or invented symbols that you make up. Ask your child to draw the OPPOSITE of each symbol.

• Set aside an evening that is to be "blackout night." Achieve a blackout either by turning off lights and unplugging appliances, or by cutting the main power supply. Let your children take the lead in suggesting how to deal with practical matters and entertainment.

• Invent humorous physical challenges for your child to undertake. (The humor encourages her to try—especially if she is sometimes fearful of learning new physical skills.) If you like, ritualize the time when this event takes place—perhaps every Saturday afternoon. These activities will enhance tolerance of ambiguity by encouraging risk-taking, delay of gratification, and respect for that important component of creativity—the willingness to be silly.

Challenges could include:

walking a balance beam (a two-by-four set on the ground) while singing a song;

riding a bike in circles without spilling a paper cup half full of water placed on the child's head;

rolling down a long hill (to get good and dizzy!) and running back up in a straight line within a certain time limit;

seeing how many ways your child can think of to make a ball go into a trash can. (For older children you can alter the size of the can or ball, as well as distance from the can, to increase the difficulty.) Set the can up on the driveway or in the basement, freestanding or against the wall.

Children can concentrate on how the ball moves (rolling off the garage roof, swishing straight in, number of bounces on the ground, number of ricochets), on devices that can be used to send the ball on its merry way (swatting it with rackets, bats, wood planks, rolling it along an old length of gutter), or on the process used by the thrower (blindfolded, backwards, through the legs, while singing "The Star-Spangled Banner," and so on).

13

WHEN THE WALLS SHAKE AND THE PLASTER FALLS: PROBLEM-SOLVING

*O*ne of us once asked a twelve-year-old girl for her definition of a problem. "A problem" she said, "is something you worry about." The beauty of this definition is that it implies a choice: you can worry and have a problem, or you can not worry and not have a problem. You may still face a challenge or a mystery—but it won't be a problem.

Nurtured children approach problem-solving with this healthy attitude. This isn't to say that they lick their chops every time something goes wrong. Rather, they understand that problems are a natural part of life. They approach them with hope for success rather than fear of failure.

One can observe natural problem-solving ability in the youngest of children—every time they figure out how to roll over, stand up, build a block tower, or open a jar. Most kids love "brain teasers." Over time, however, as children are accused of being silly for coming up with harebrained solutions or chastised for being wrong, most kids' enjoyment of problem-solving erodes.

Many different models have been presented by researchers to explain the problem-solving process. While these models differ in terminology and numbers of mental steps involved, they do share certain similarities. Basically, all models contain an initial stage in which the existence of a problem is sensed or observed. At this point, the problem must be understood and properly defined. Improper identification, or denial that a problem exists, can lead the process astray at this stage. Next comes a period in which ideas and possible solutions are gathered. A process of analysis is then engaged in which options are evaluated and consequences considered. Modifications and new ideas may enter into the pot at this time. Finally a decision is made and a course of action selected. The solution is implemented. Fine-tuning and reevaluation may occur to achieve ultimate resolution.

We asked the parents in our study how they solved problems at home. "How do we solve problems?" one parent responded. "I don't know. We just solve them. Things happen, we talk about them, we come up with ideas, we figure something out."

At first glance, this parent's comment seems too broad to contain any useful advice. Upon closer inspection, it's amazing how succinctly it summarizes the basic four steps of problem-solving:

1. recognizing and defining the problem;
2. generating possible solutions;
3. analyzing options;
4. choosing and implementing a plan.

Many problems get solved without any consciousness of a process: a child tries to reach the cookie jar on a top shelf; a teenager is bent on redecorating her room. In each case a goal appears, ideas for implementing it are considered, and a course of action is engaged (and possibly adjusted as new input redefines the best route to success). Perhaps because it is a "happy" problem, it is unlikely, and unnecessary, that the "actor" see herself as being in a problem-solving mode. At other times, however, we are quite conscious of having activated a process in order to deal with an obstacle or task. This might occur when we look for a new job, or figure out how we're going to meet some large, unanticipated expense.

The four-step model is useful for conceptualizing how nurturing parents facilitate their children's problem-solving skills. The suggestions we present can be used equally well for group problem-solving by the entire family, or for personal problem-solving.

1. RECOGNIZING AND DEFINING THE PROBLEM

Many problems never get solved for the simple reason that their existence is never acknowledged. This can be the result of denial or inattention. In some cases, one may recognize a problem, but may choose, for a variety of reasons, not to deal with it:

"I just don't have the time right now."

"It's not worth the risk."

"I can stand it for a couple more months."

In other cases, problems will disappear as the natural result of passing time, developmental growth, or changing events and circumstances. In families, however, far too many conflicts are allowed to fester, poisoning relationships and siphoning off emotional energy. Even if the existence of a problem is recognized, things can still go wrong at this stage by incorrectly defining it; neither the doctor nor the auto mechanic can fix a thing if they've misdiagnosed the problem.

Nurturing parents avoid these pitfalls. They pick up problems early because they are sensitive to family mood and to the needs and feelings of their children. They approach conflict nonjudgmentally, and the base line of good communication and trust they have established with their children maximizes the likelihood that problems can be discussed and correctly identified.

Several parents spoke about the importance of this issue. "My son," said one father, "likes to play his stereo so that the walls shake and the plaster falls. But the problem isn't that he does that; the problem is that I can't stand it. Does that make any sense?" Other parents nodded. "What I'm trying to say is that my response is just as much a factor in the problem as is his action. Don't get me wrong—I'm not denying that kids can be inconsiderate, but if I weren't home, or if he blasted the house with Vivaldi's *Four Seasons* instead of some psychopathic heavy metal, the problem would disappear or change. So when I go to my son's room, it's not to tell him that he's 'bad' or 'wrong' or listens to lousy music. It's to tell him that I can't concentrate. That's the problem. And I think the fact that I approach it that way is why he instantly says, 'Sorry, Dad,' and turns it down. Maybe I'm making a big deal out of a little distinction, but I think how a problem gets framed is a big factor in how it gets solved."

How a problem gets framed *is* a big deal. Too often, family problems are defined as residing in, or being created by, the child. This narrow definition places an unfair onus on the child, and children know it. No wonder they resist when 100 percent of the "blame" is placed on their shoulders. Why should *they* be the only ones to change?

The parents in our study intuitively recognize that it takes two to tangle. When responsibility for a problem is laid across many shoulders, solutions become easier, not harder. Parents and children can work as equal partners in affecting a solution. Change is motivated by a desire to be considerate and to respect everyone's rights. It would be hard to imagine a more powerful and moral force at work on behalf of family harmony.

This final example illustrates, from another angle, how important it is to define a problem accurately. "My daughter came to me a few weeks ago. 'My allowance isn't big enough,' she said. I let her talk for a while and then suggested that what I heard her saying wasn't that her allowance wasn't big enough, but that *she needed more money*. That's quite a different problem. It allows for many more solutions than just whether I raise her allowance or not. If she needs more money we can consider loaning it to her, or she might sell some of her things, get a job, cut her expenses, or offer to do work around the house."

There are several things parents can do to facilitate this initial recognition stage of the problem-solving process:

Be explicit. If there's a problem, acknowledge it. "Guys, I think we've got a problem here." "I want to bring up something that's been bothering me." "Things don't seem to be working well." "There's a family issue we need to discuss."

The most critical thing at this stage is to be nonaccusative. Avoid placing blame and putting kids on the defensive. Why should kids participate in a discussion if it's already been decided that they're at fault? At the beginning, state problems as broadly and nonjudgmentally as possible. Better yet, let your kids define the problem. You might be surprised how different things look from their perspective. The following examples show the difference between accusative and nonaccusative framing of a problem:

Accusative	Nonaccusative
You kids are lazy, ungrateful, and irresponsible, and you aren't doing your fair share around the house.	I've noticed that chores haven't been getting done around here. I want to talk about it with you.

Susie hogs the phone and nobody can use it and my friends can never get through and it isn't *fay-aire*!	My friends have said that they can never reach me at night because the phone is busy.

Don't confuse symptoms with problems. Dig deeply. A child's behavior is often merely a clue that something else is troubling him. The real source of the trouble may have very little to do with the surface indication. For example, a child's aggression or hostility in school may be labeled "the problem," when actually the core problem is a learning disability, or a hearing loss.

Let your children know that problems are natural and inevitable. Sometimes, kids are afraid to share their concerns because they don't want to appear weak or incapable. They don't want to disappoint parental expectations. Reassure your children that their problems do not reflect on their worthiness as people. You love them, problems and all.

2. GENERATING POSSIBLE SOLUTIONS

Even the most well-defined problem will persist if there are no ideas for how to solve it. Two of the greatest blocks to problem-solving at this stage are functional fixity and judgmental environments. The first is a sort of mental strait-jacket which limits the production of ideas by constricting the mind's movement; the second achieves the same end by inhibiting the risk-taking and self-confidence essential to creativity.

We spoke earlier of functional fixity rather literally; as children learn about how things work (from machines to social interactions), functions tend to become fixed in their minds, and they are often unable to imagine things being any other way. Functional fixity, however, can also occur in problem-solving methods themselves. Luchins (1952) demonstrated this with his now famous water jar experiment:

The Luchins Water Jar Problem
DIRECTIONS: For each problem, use the empty water jars indicated in columns A, B, and C as measures to obtain the amount of

water in column D. Fill jar D as efficiently as possible. That is, use jars A, B, and C as little as possible to obtain the exact amount in jar D.

Use These Jars as Measures to Fill Jar D
with Water (Numbers refer to ounces
each jar measures)

Problem	A	B	C	Required Water D
1.	3	29	3	20
2.	21	127	3	100
3.	14	163	25	99
4.	18	43	10	5
5.	9	42	6	21
6.	20	59	4	31
7.	23	49	3	20
8.	15	39	3	18
9.	28	76	3	42
10.	18	48	4	22

By the time you got to the sixth problem, you probably had devised a solution that amounts to this formula: $B - A - 2C = D$; you would be right. This formula also works for the remaining four problems, and if you are like most people, you went right on using it. But for three of these last four problems (problems 7, 8, and 10), there are much simpler formulas:

Problem 7 can be solved by $A - C = D$
Problems 8 and 10 can be solved by $A + C = D$

If you noticed this, you are much less functionally fixed than most people.

Fluency—the ability to generate many ideas (see Chapter 8)—can often be used to work through the block of functional fixity. Cognitive psychologist Karl Dunker (1945) designed an exercise that demonstrates how this can be done:

A person has an inoperable tumor in his stomach. There are rays that can destroy the tumor, but they will also destroy surrounding tissue if turned up strong enough to kill the tumor.

How, then, can one safely destroy the tumor? Dunker took the phrase "take a ray" and combined it with forty-two prepositions to look at possible relationships between rays. Some of the combinations he came up with were:

Take a ray about a ray
Take a ray across a ray
Take a ray after a ray
Take a ray against a ray
Take a ray among a ray

Some of the sentences obviously make no sense. One does, though—take a ray across a ray—and it offers a solution:

> *One ray is beamed through the stomach at an intensity just low enough so that it cannot damage tissue. Another ray of the same intensity is beamed from another angle, so that one beam flows across the other (take a ray across a ray) at the location of the tumor. Their combined strength is enough to destroy the tumor. There, and only there, the tissue is destroyed.*

A child's ability to generate ideas is influenced by both mental and emotional factors. Functional freedom, originality, and good communication between the right and left sides of the brain are of little value to the child if an oppressive environment inhibits their use. Nothing thwarts the risk-taking and free association necessary to problem-solving more quickly than a critical atmosphere. Go back to your own schooldays. . . .

> *You're sitting in class. The teacher asks a question. The answer pops into your head. I've got it, you think. All around you is silence. Nobody moves. Nobody responds. I'm right. I'm sure I have the right answer. Yet something prevents you from raising your hand. Maybe I'm not right. How come no one else is raising their hand? But I know I'm right. Well, I think I'm right. I guess maybe I might be wrong. I better not say anything. I might be wrong. The teacher breaks the si-*

lence by giving the answer. I was right! I did know it. Why didn't I say anything?

You didn't say anything because the environment inhibited risk-taking and creative expression. Your fear of being wrong was greater than your conviction of being right. This authoritarian context invariably hinders problem-solving, particularly at the idea-generating stage. A model for problem-solving does exist, however. This model creates the democratic, accepting climate most conducive to the production of ideas.

BRAINSTORMING

First developed by Alex Osborn (1963), an executive of a major New York advertising firm, brainstorming is a technique designed to help small groups produce high-quality ideas. It is based on the concept that the production of ideas should be kept separate from the evaluation of their worth. Osborn had observed that most conferences, which are based on the principles of debate, seldom hatch creative solutions. In such meetings, criticism of the participants' thoughts plays a large role. This holds true for "conferences" between parents and children where, too often, the focus is on labeling and maligning the other's point of view. No wonder typical family arguments rarely solve problems; nothing in the process aims at *solving*.

Brainstorming techniques, however, provide parents and children with a set of guidelines which can be used to address problems in a constructive, nonjudgmental climate:

1. The problem, need, or issue is stated in a nonaccusatory manner.
2. Everyone is invited to contribute ideas. Production of a large quantity of ideas is encouraged.

> Suggestions are tape recorded or jotted down by a group secretary.
> *No criticism of ideas is permitted.* Often a leader is chosen whose job it is to ring a bell if any criticism occurs.

Participants strive to avoid editing their own ideas, consciously or unconsciously. (This can be quite difficult; we are conditioned to label and prejudge our ideas as stupid, naive, or impractical.)

Wild, funny, or even silly ideas are welcome. They frequently spawn high-quality thoughts. (This means that even very young children can play a valuable and equal role in brainstorming.)

Building on the contributions of others is encouraged.

3.   When the group feels that it has exhausted all the possibilities, suggestions are discussed and evaluated. (Convergent thinking takes the place of divergent thinking.)

4.   A solution or course of action is chosen, ideally by consensus. Methods for follow-up and/or reevaluation are set.

Brainstorming encourages fluency, originality, androgyny, risk-taking, tolerance of ambiguity, and stimulus and functional freedom. It is a creative and democratic method for problem-solving. Obviously there is a self-consciousness to the process, but sometimes a formal meeting is an ideal way for families to address problems and decisions. Nurturing parents, however, tend to use the principles of this method informally and intuitively. They encourage their children to do the same with their own problems.

"My daughter came to me quite upset the other day," said one of the mothers in our study. "She had accepted an invitation to go to a dance with a boy at school, having decided that the boy she really liked wasn't going to ask her. Well, the next day, of course, he does. She put him off without giving a definite answer. I asked her what she planned to do. 'I don't know,' she said. She was concerned that by going with the first boy the second would think she wasn't interested. Yet she had agreed to go. I suggested she try to think of as many ways to deal with it as possible. I was amazed at what she came up with: lies, charades, disguises, secret notes, heart-to-heart talks, suicide, entering a convent. We both knew some of the ideas were ridiculous, but somehow, saying them and discarding them helped to clarify what was important to her."

"Don't leave us hanging. What did she decide?" asked the other parents.

"Oh," laughed the mother. "She decided that she had to go with the first boy since she had already accepted his invitation. But she would give her regrets to the second boy with as much encouragement as possible without telling him outright that she wished she was going with him because that might get back to the first boy and make him feel bad. You *know* how delicate these things can be! She ended up having a wonderful time with the first boy, and now her new problem is that she doesn't know who she likes better!"

There are several things parents can do to assist their children at this idea-generating stage of problem-solving:

Have your child divide problems into parts. An overwhelming obstacle can become quite manageable if it is taken one step at a time, one day at a time. Focus brainstorming on the highest priority or the most immediate issue.

Think of opposites of solutions.

In his book *New Think*, Edward de Bono makes a distinction between vertical thinking (which means ideas that move in a straight line between lower- and higher-level concepts) and lateral thinking (which means looking for alternate ways of defining or interpreting a problem). He states, "Vertical thinking digs the same hole deeper; lateral thinking is concerned with digging a hole in another place."

Vertical thinking plays an essential role in creativity, but if the hole is in the wrong place, then no amount of logic is going to put it in the right place.

Encourage your children to "dig holes" in new places:

- Come up with silly, crazy ideas yourself.
- Tell your kids to forget that old rule, *Think before you speak*. In a brainstorm, *Speak before you think* is the order of the day.
- Reverse roles. Suggest that everyone pretend they're ten years older, or that it's one hundred years ago, or that they're someone other than themselves (a sibling, a teacher, a friend, a hero). In that new guise, come up with ideas.

3. ANALYZING OPTIONS

By this point in the process, the problem is well-defined, and a long list of possible solutions is ready for evaluation. Parents and children should be aware, however, of a number of pitfalls which can occur at this analysis stage:

People with low tolerance of ambiguity may be in a rush to end the uncertainty created by unsolved problems. This can lead to a failure to consider adequately the consequences of various courses of action.

Judgment can creep back into the process and poison the congenial and creative atmosphere.

It's possible that in spite of a long list of ideas, the "right" one isn't there yet.

Parents can keep problem-solving on a healthy course by following these guidelines:

Let your children do the evaluating. Ask them what they think of the ideas. Which ones look promising? Which ones should be discarded? Keep the evaluation centered on the merits of each idea. Avoid the sort of labeling that hurts feelings. If children lead the analysis, it becomes a positive process in which the focus is not on the rejection of their ideas, but on the quality of their thinking.

Be aware of everyone's defensiveness. Even unconsciously, people want their own ideas to "win." Certain solutions unavoidably direct attention to some family members more than to others, possibly implying fault or responsibility. These factors can bias the analysis phase of problem-solving. The best way to minimize the chances of this happening is to keep everyone focused on the future: "There's nothing we can do about the past. Let's just make sure things will work better from now on." Of course, sometimes problem-solving has to include a detour into the past—to undo damage, correct a wrong, or identify an error—but the whole point is to allow everyone, victim and perpetrator alike, to move ahead.

Another way to check for possible defensiveness is to get feedback from those who are less personally involved. We do this naturally every time we consult a spouse, colleague, or friend. Children can be encouraged to test possible solutions by talking with their peers, relatives, or teachers.

Avoid the temptation of latching on to easy, logical solutions that just won't work because they fly in the face of everyone's experience. For instance, if a child's phone calls average an hour each, be suspicious of a solution that suddenly requires her to limit them to five minutes. If a solution demands that a child pay for half of something, does the child have the financial where-withal to do so?

Be willing to return to the idea-generating stage to modify ideas that seem to hold potential. A mini-brainstorm can flesh out promising leads.

In the process of evaluating possible solutions, it may become clear that you just haven't hit upon the right idea yet. Don't worry. Most problems will wait patiently. Don't rush toward a solution just to be "done" with the problem. Let ideas incubate. Many of us have had the experience of being stymied by some problem that requires a creative solution. Frustrated, we give up and go to a movie, mow the lawn, or take a nap. Suddenly, hours or days later, the solution pops up, seemingly out of nowhere. This is an ex-ample of what is called the "incubation stage" of the creative process: we leave the problem alone while previous efforts to solve it are allowed to sink into the unconscious mind. If ideas seem slow in coming, "Why don't we sleep on it," can be won-derful advice. Tomorrow may bring fresh insight. (We know of one rather sophisticated youth who, when asked by his father why he was watching television instead of doing his homework, re-plied, "I'm incubating, Dad.")

4. CHOOSING AND IMPLEMENTING A PLAN

If the first three stages of problem-solving have been approached with integrity, the chances are excellent that a high-level, creative solution is at hand. Because of its high quality, though, the chosen solution may not be the safest or most typical scenario. Following through could mean taking a risk, sticking up for one's principles, or making a sacrifice. This can be difficult for children. Now, more than ever, they need their parents' trust and backing. It is very easy, once a problem is "solved," to assume that it is over. Yet additional consequences may ensue from the problem-solving strategy itself. Feelings and relationships may continue to be affected. New issues may develop.

The girl who didn't know which boy to go to the dance with was still enmeshed in the problem even after she had decided what to do. In this final stage of selection, implementation, and follow-through, parents can continue to support their children:

Without being judgmental, try to express confidence in your child's ability to pull off his decision. Don't, however, minimize the effort involved or give the impression that you take your child's success for granted. When parents "know" that their child will succeed, when they expect nothing less, a double message is conveyed—one of confidence, yes, but also one of destiny, as if success resides outside of the child, and will accrue to him by divine right. This suggestion that success is ordained (by being his parents' offspring) rather than earned (by the child's hard work) can unintentionally diminish his confidence in his own powers.

Many problems require ongoing efforts to maintain a solution: a child adhering to a study schedule or trying to gain better control of her temper, a family using a new system for chores, a set of siblings sharing use of a kids' telephone. Stay tuned in to the situation. Ask your kids how it's going, if any new problems have come up, or whether they've had to modify their original solution. Your continued interest will help to keep their motivation high.

THE FOUR-STEP STRATEGY DOESN'T *ALWAYS* WORK

A child's "problems" can range from a broken pencil to a playground bully, from a book report to a falling out with a friend, from a misplaced assignment to a paralyzing injury. Similarly, the issues and conflicts families face range from humorous to heartrending, from trivial to tragic. We don't want to leave the impression that all problems can be neatly solved by a four-step strategy. Sometimes, there is no solution—just a set of unhappy choices to be made, the lesser of two evils to be selected. In many cases, however, parents and children can grab a toehold to control the events and relationships that affect their lives. They can use problem-solving as a means of growing and understanding.

Warmth, respect, and trust build the nonjudgmental atmosphere in which problem-solving flourishes. Children who are raised by nurturing parents are particularly good problem-solvers because they are able to tolerate and enjoy ambiguity, delay gratification, take risks, and consider options androgynously. These strengths are complemented by stimulus and functional freedom, originality, and self-control. In fact, nowhere do the ten personality traits support each other more visibly than in the area of problem-solving. As nurturing parents engage their children in activities that foster these traits, they are inculcating problem-solving skills that their children can put to use at school, in social relationships, and in later life.

ACTIVITIES TO NURTURE PROBLEM-SOLVING

WHO CAN FIND THE RAISIN?

Materials: two cups (that you can't see through); raisins or similar snack; cardboard shapes: triangles, circles and squares—each in three different sizes and two different colors for a total of eighteen cut-outs; each big enough to cover the top of the cup.

For one- to two-year-olds, start simply. Without your child watching, place a raisin in one of the cups and cover it with a cardboard square. Cover the empty cup with a circle of the same size and color. Ask your child to guess which cup has the raisin in it. If he's right, he gets the raisin as his prize. If he guesses wrong, remove the cups from his sight, and then replace them in reversed position, keeping the raisin in its original cup under the square. Continue until your child recognizes the pattern—that the raisin is always in the cup under the square. Once he clearly has the hang of it, but before his interest wanes, present a new pattern for him to discover: the raisin is always under the circle, or under the blue shape, or under the smaller of the two shapes. If your child gets so good at this game that the raisins threaten to spoil his appetite for dinner, it's time to stop.

Extensions:

As your child gets older you can increase the complexity of the game. Use more cups, more shapes, and/or more colors to create more combinations. Set up new categories to make it harder for your child to discern the pattern: the raisin is always in the cup between two circles, or to the right of any square, or maybe it's a pattern of movement—the raisin keeps "moving" to the next cup on the left. When you think that your child has figured it out, ask him to verbalize the principle he used to locate the raisin.

SORTING SHAPES

Materials: Take three lengths of string at least four feet long and tie the two ends of each length together in order to make three string circles. You also need nine cardboard shapes: three squares, three triangles, three circles. Make one set white, one black, and one striped (See figure 13.1 on page 182).

Lay the string circles on the floor. Overlap two of the circles.

Place all the triangles in one of the two overlapping circles. Place all the striped shapes in the other. Explain to your child that she should put into the area of overlap any shapes that "belong" there. The area that overlaps is the place where shapes should be added that have characteristics satisfying the conditions of *both* circles. In this case, the striped triangle would go in the overlap, since the attributes "striped" and "triangle" are compatible with both circles. (The "outside" circle is the place where the remaining pieces go.)

As in Who Can Find the Raisin, you are creating situations where your child must mentally test patterns in order to arrive at a solution. If she gets stuck and can't figure out which pieces go into the overlap and which belong in the "outside" circle, give her an explanation and go on to a new setup.

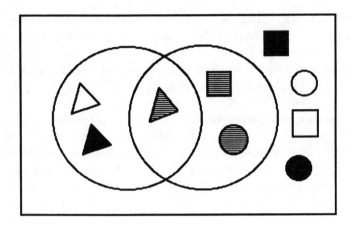

Figure 13.1: The Sorting Shapes Game

Extensions:

Once you think you're up to it, increase the complexity of the game. Add a fourth circle so that you can have three circles overlapping. Add more shapes in different colors and sizes to multiply the permutations. Get older siblings involved, especially if they've studied Venn diagrams in math. They can be the ones to invent the setups!

MAKE A HYPOTHESIS

Materials: two sheets of 10-×-10-inch white paper ruled into 1-inch squares (the one hundred squares should be numbered consecutively, horizontally or vertically—it doesn't matter); three crayons: one yellow, one orange, one red.

Explain to your child that a *hypothesis* is a reasoned guess. Then tell your child that he is going to take the checkered sheet of paper to at least fifty people and ask them to select a square randomly. Ideally there should be an equal number of right- and left-handed subjects. But first, ask your child to construct a hypothesis as to which squares most people will choose, and whether he thinks there will be any difference between right- and left-handers.

As he collects his data, he needs to note the number of the square each person chooses, and whether that person is right- or left-handed. When he finishes the survey, have him color in the two sheets as follows (one is to record the right-handers' responses, the other is for the left-handers' responses):

Squares that nobody selected	leave the square WHITE
Squares that ONE person selected	color YELLOW
Squares that TWO people selected	color ORANGE
Squares that THREE or MORE people selected	color RED

The darkest area for right-handers is likely to be in the center of the RIGHT half of the sheet, reflecting the right bias and the tendency of most people to stay away from the edge. Left-handers' selections are likely to be centered on the LEFT half of the sheet for similar reasons. Have your child and any other children who take part in the survey discuss their hypotheses and results. Draw out their findings, their discrepancies, and their theories for why things happened the way they did. This exercise sharpens their ability to make predictions, and then test them out with real data. Both skills are critical to problem-solving.

Extensions:

Repeat the survey but alter the testing conditions. Ask your child to make new hypotheses. For example, would the results change if subjects had to POINT to the square of their choice using their UNFAVORED hand, or if they were told that the sheet of paper represents the ocean and the square they choose is the island on which they are marooned? Does it matter whether it's the Atlantic or Pacific Ocean?

Have your kids dream up new research studies, make hypotheses, and test them in real life. This activity is great for building social skills, too.

OTHER ACTIVITIES:

• Present your child with several empty jars. Tell him that his job is to use them to make a musical instrument. The only guideline you should offer is that the jars may not be broken. If he seems stumped, suggest that he experiment with filling the jars. Different levels of water do the trick.

• Place a penny in the bottom of an empty widemouthed bottle while the bottle is standing in an upright position. Tell your child that it is her job to get the penny out of the bottle without touching or moving the bottle. Putting some chewing gum on the end of a stick and pressing it onto the penny is one way to solve the problem.

• Talk to your child about the notion of camouflage clothing. Present him with the challenge of creating an appearance that somehow blends with his surroundings. Starting with some old clothes, have him (and a friend if he wishes) create camouflage clothing for an outdoor location. This could be a nearby woods, a corner of the backyard, or even a spot in front of a building or store. Another challenge would be to create clothing to camouflage his presence in the house. When he is ready to test his cover, have him hide while you and others try to find him.

• Arrange twenty pennies in a straight line. Each of the players takes a turn, in which they remove either one or two pennies from the line. The problem is to decide how many pennies to take on each turn (depending on what one's opponent does), so that another player will be forced to take the last penny and so lose the game.

• Show your child two glass containers, one filled with water and the other with cooking oil. Have him drop a teaspoon of sand into each container. Ask him to explain what has just happened. Encourage him to try different liquids, to drop different substances into them, and to explain the results. We recommend a supervising parent in order to prevent those experiments in which Mommy's earrings and Daddy's cuff links are dropped in paint remover and indelible India ink.

14

FINDING THE TEACHER YOU WISH YOU HAD: THE NURTURING SCHOOL

*A*s the headmaster of a school for eleven- to fifteen-year-olds, one of the authors of this book frequently met with parents wishing to enroll their children. The school offered an alternative program which, along with other goals, placed great emphasis on developing responsibility, creativity, and empathy. We would call it a nurturing school. Because of the school's unique nature, some of the kids it attracted had been labeled as "troublemakers." Their parents were desperate. They spoke of children who were scared or scarred; children who had lost spirit and self-confidence, who no longer found interest or joy in learning.

"I don't know what to do. Every morning my daughter cries and says she doesn't want to go to school. I have to force her out the door."

"Peter simply will not do his homework. We've tried everything—threats, punishments, rewards, tutors—but nothing works."

"Megan used to be so curious about everything. Now she just seems bored."

"I've been down to the principal's office five times this month. If it isn't a fight, he's cut class or talked back to his teacher."

"I guess I have what's known as a problem child."

Each case was examined carefully, and in some cases, these parents were told, "No, you don't have a problem child, you have a problem school. The fact that your child is unhappy and acting out is a sign of health! He's fighting back against an unhealthy environment." And indeed, within a few short weeks of leaving their old, un-nurturing schools, virtually all of these "problem" kids blossomed into happy, cooperative, and motivated human beings.

In this chapter we look at nurturing child-raising in the larger context of school experiences. We examine the relationship between a school's philosophy and structure, and a child's creativity, responsibility, and empathy. What happens when children raised in a nurturing home go to school? Are the values of most schools compatible with the values of this parenting style? The answer, sadly, is no. This doesn't mean, however, that these children can't enjoy school and do well in it. But it does mean that parents need to know how to protect their children from this type of cultural assault, and how to find those schools and teachers that support the values of the nurturing home.

Based upon their personality traits, we would expect nurtured kids to embrace the unknown with curiosity and excitement—and they do! Because they are tolerant of ambiguity, they can hardly wait for that first day of school, when a wonderful new world beckons them to explore, learn, and grow. So far so good. As time goes on, however, many of these children, by virtue of their *strengths*, will begin to chafe at the methods, attitudes, and goals that characterize many schools and teachers. This happens for one simple reason: most schools emphasize the three Rs: Rules, Report Cards, and Regurgitation. No wonder studies show a marked decrease in creative problem-solving abilities with each year that children spend in school! It is ironic that our educational institutions, in teaching young people to contribute to society, strip them of the very qualities that contribute the most.

Why should this be so? The answers become clear if we look more closely at the effects of schooling on creativity, responsibility, and empathy.

THE EFFECTS OF SCHOOLING ON CREATIVITY

Educator Ralph Hallman (1967) suggests that these obstacles to creative problem-solving are typical of most school systems:

1. *Pressure to conform.* Probably the major inhibitor, this involves standardized routines, inflexible rules, and squelching of individual expression.

2. *Ridicule of unusual ideas.* This destroys self-confidence and molds thinking into a search for right answers.

3. *An excessive quest for success and the rewards it brings.* This distorts learning into an externally motivated process in which the child tries to meet the standards and demands of others to obtain the rewards they have to give. The intrinsic motivation required for creativity is destroyed.

4. *Intolerance of a playful attitude.* Innovation calls for playing around with ideas, a willingness to fantasize, and a healthy disrespect for accepted concepts. As Hallman remarks, "Creativity is profound fun." Many schools act as if learning and fun are mutually exclusive.

In Chapter 4, the Two-String Test revealed the effects of education on functional freedom. Ninety percent of sixth graders studied could solve the problem within the fifteen minutes allotted. Only 20 percent of the graduate students studied achieved a solution!

In the study mentioned earlier (Dacey and Ripple, 1967), the creative abilities of twelve-hundred seventh and eighth graders in forty-five school systems were studied. One of the main instruments was the Story-Writing Test described in Chapter 5. The results of this test are charted in Figure 14.1. As you can see, the largest group of students scored in the bottom third of the possible range of scores. Such a finding is surprising since it is known that almost all human traits and abilities (IQ, height, weight, watermelon-seed spitting) are "normally distributed." Most people are average, with only a few getting the lowest and highest scores. A normal distribution of scores thus produces a bell-shaped curve on a graph. Figure 14.2 illustrates such a curve for the distribution of IQ scores for Americans.

So why are the creativity scores shown in Figure 14.1 distributed so differently? One obvious hypothesis would be that this reflects genetic inheritance; most people inherit only a little creative ability, and a few lucky people inherit a lot. There are several problems with this explanation. For one thing, it does not explain why creativity should be different from all the other normally distributed traits. In addition, there is little evidence that creativity is so highly influenced by genes.

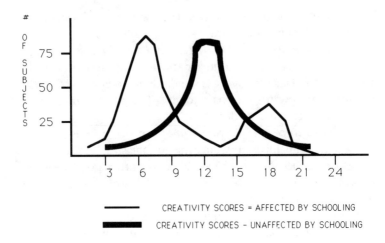

CREATIVITY SCORES = AFFECTED BY SCHOOLING
CREATIVITY SCORES – UNAFFECTED BY SCHOOLING

Figure 14.1: The Effect of Schooling on Creativity Score

What if, however, at birth, creativity is naturally distributed just like IQ, but then is adversely affected by some major experience such as attending school? Such an effect could, over time, move everyone's score lower on the graph. It would not affect the *shape*

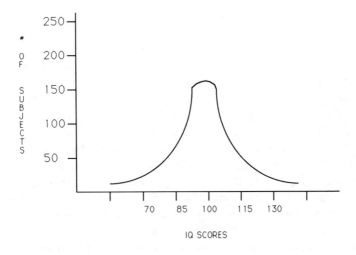

IQ SCORES

Figure 14.2: The Normal Distribution of IQ scores

of the distribution—which would still be bell-shaped—but it would drop everyone's average. Let us suppose further that the stifling effect of schooling is powerful enough to affect most students—the bottom three-quarters. Those in the top quarter are impervious to the effect—they go on being creative no matter how they are treated by the school system, because they have such independent personalities. If this were the case, we would get a curve much like the one we see in Figure 14.1. The hypothesis that creativity is adversely affected by schooling was considered to be the most likely explanation for the unusual results.

Psychologist E. P. Torrance (1982) found evidence not only that creativity is squelched by schooling, but that it happens to girls more quickly than it does to boys. He measured the creative abilities of first graders by asking them to suggest how three toys could be improved so that they would be more fun to play with. The toys were a fire truck (considered a boy's toy), a nurse's kit (considered a girl's toy), and a stuffed dog (considered neutral at this age). The responses were scored according to fluency (total number of ideas), flexibility (the number of ideas that were qualitatively different from each other), and originality (the number of ideas that no one else in the group had thought of).

The average scores broke down as would be expected: boys' scores in each of the category types were higher than girls' for the fire truck; girls' were similarly superior to boys' for the nurse's kit; and the two sexes did about equally well with the stuffed dog.

Torrance administered the test two years later, when the children were about to enter the third grade. The change was striking: the boys' scores were superior to those of the girls on *all* of the toys, including the nurse's kit! On the basis of many discussions with teachers, Torrance concluded that sex role identification was the cause of such a rapid decline; that girls in elementary school are likely to be reinforced for "ladylike" behavior—demureness and acquiescence—by their mostly female teachers. These attributes inhibit creative growth. Boys, on the other hand, are allowed to be more active, aggressive, and questioning. Thus, their creativity is beaten down more slowly.

Another element responsible for the deadening effect of schooling on creativity may be deduced from some well-known research carried out by T. W. Adorno (1950) and others. They devised a test for "authoritarianism." They knew that people who have this personality characteristic become quite angry when those in an "inferior" position fail to behave in a subservient way. Authoritarians want instant obedience from those "below" them. These researchers were surprised to learn from their studies that authoritarian people also feel that *they* should be subservient to those they perceive as being above them. Thus the "authoritarian" is someone who has an exaggerated sense of social hierarchies, or "pecking orders." Dominance and subordination are key factors in life for them.

Adorno's authoritarianism test was administered to hundreds of persons in nearly four hundred American occupations. Guess what job came out on top? No, not teachers. The number one spot for authoritarian types went to state police, followed closely by army officers (soldiers in general were in the bottom half). Teachers were third!

Let's look first at what state police and army officers have in common. Among their mutual trademarks:

Both bear arms and are allowed by society to use them to enforce orders.

Both wear uniforms that have abundant signs of rank: collar pins, arm patches, hat bands, and medals.

Both have court systems, whether public or military, that deal out punishments when orders are disobeyed.

Both have traditions by which those in inferior stations are generally required to salute or otherwise recognize higher-ranking officers. (Saluting developed in medieval Europe, when the serfs were forced to grasp the forelocks of their hair and pull their heads down, as a gesture of respect for the lord of the manor as he rode around inspecting his fields.)

Both make heavy use of "sir" when addressing male superiors. (This practice also derives from the medieval world. "Sire" was the term for addressing lords.)

Teachers, of course, are totally different from police and military officers. Or are they? Consider these characteristics of the teaching profession:

Under a mandate of serving and protecting, teachers are vested with near total authority over their pupils. They are able to deal out punishments and turn students over to higher commands of authority. Corporal punishment of schoolchildren is legal in most of the United States. It is actively practiced in many!

The entire educational system is based on rules and regulations, curriculum manuals, hierarchies, promotions, and rewards and punishments.

There is an implied if not explicit pecking order that locates students, teachers, and administrators on a power map.

Many schools have prisonlike atmospheres with police or security personnel in evidence, grates on windows, and barred or locked doors. Indiscriminate searches of students' persons and property have been upheld by courts.

Permission must be obtained by students to speak and move about.

Physical order is valued and maintained: single file, no talking, face forward, forward march!

Admittedly this is a one-sided portrait. The teaching profession is full of loving, dedicated, inspiring, creative people—underpaid and underappreciated—who literally and figuratively save lives every day. But it also includes many people who, consciously or not, come to the profession because of authoritarian personality characteristics. At some point or another, we all had teachers of this type. They are hazardous to a nurtured child's health.

THE EFFECTS OF SCHOOLING ON RESPONSIBILITY

The philosophy of most conventional schools is to teach by telling. Responsibility, however, cannot be taught in such a way. It would be like trying to teach swimming in a classroom. One learns to swim by getting in the water. According to the famous educator John Dewey (1975), "The only way to prepare for social life is to engage in social life. . . . The child cannot get power of judgment excepting as he is continually experimenting in forming judgments. He must have an opportunity to select for himself."

This, of course, is the approach taken by nurturing parents. They provide their children with opportunities to select for themselves—to develop responsibility by being responsible. This endowment of respect and support motivates high levels of behavior.

Children in most schools, however, are endowed, not with respect and trust, but with lavatory passes and rule books. One group of researchers discovered a school with over one hundred formal and informal rules! Many of these rules exist for the convenience of teachers and administrators. They reflect adult mistrust and fear of loss of control; they are often arbitrary, and arguably unconstitutional (for example, locker searches or indiscriminate drug testing). Nor are the rules open to debate or change: "If I made an exception for you, I'd have to make an exception for everybody." In that these rules are often unfeeling and unfair, and in that they are imposed from above without the consent of the governed, they do nothing to nurture student responsibility. Indeed, such a rule-driven climate—reflecting the abuses of the fewer misbehaving students at the expense of the well-behaved majority—more typically leads to teacher demoralization and student disrespect.

In typical schools, the reward for responsible behavior is simply the absence of trouble. That, however, is the same outcome enjoyed by students who break rules—provided they don't get caught. Thus, the hidden message is that it is *perception* of behavior, rather than behavior itself, that determines consequences. A parallel to this can be seen in grading systems that reward children for right answers and "punish" them for wrong ones: it is the *perception* of learning, rather than learning itself, that matters. The "A" gets the prize, regardless of how it was obtained. No wonder 95 percent of high school juniors and seniors admit to cheating in school.

A number of studies have compared traditional public high schools with alternative public high schools in areas of student behavior, attitudes, and moral reasoning. Such comparisons are of interest to us in that they essentially compare authoritarian and nurturing approaches to education. The authoritarian stance taken by most traditional schools can be seen in features such as these:

- emphasis on rules, obedience, and conformity;
- reliance on extrinsic motivators to control behavior;
- sharp limits on student autonomy;
- role-defined student-teacher relationships;
- emphasis on product over process;
- power and decision-making vested in a small number of adults.

The nurturing nature of the alternative schools studied is evidenced by:

- increased opportunities for students to exercise responsibility;
- close, generally informal teacher-student relationships;
- democratic decision-making procedures;
- flexible scheduling;
- emphasis on curriculum relevance and independent study;
- heightened sense of community and shared values;
- broader institutional and faculty role definitions encompassing social and emotional as well as academic needs of students.

The incidence of behavior problems in these two types of schools would be one way to measure the responsibility of their students. When researchers did just that, they found that teachers and students reported far fewer behavior problems in the alternative schools as compared to the regular high schools (Duke and Perry, 1978). For example, none of the students and teachers felt that disrespect to teachers was a cause for concern in the alternative school, while 89 percent felt it was a cause for concern at the nearby high school. Twenty-six percent of students and teachers felt that disrespect to peers was a cause for concern in the alternative school; 85 percent felt it was a cause for concern at the high school. Similar disparities were expressed regarding behaviors such as vandalism, theft, fighting, classroom disruption, racial friction, and gang activity.

In another study (Kohlberg et al., 1975), the late Harvard psychologist Lawrence Kohlberg and his associates established the Just Community School, an alternative school based upon Kohlberg's cognitive-developmental theories of moral reasoning. The purpose of the school was "to develop moral reasoning by creating a school community that is perceived as fair and just by students and staff."

Kohlberg identified a number of direct and indirect conditions necessary for moral growth. Direct conditions include:

- opportunities for students to discuss and role-play issues of fairness and moral complexity;
- active participation in decisions involving moral issues;
- exposure to the next higher stage of moral reasoning.

Indirect conditions include:

- a democratic mode of operation;
- a belief that rules are fair and fairly made;
- a sense of community represented by group concern for the individual, and individual concern for the group.

In a later study, Ann Higgins and others (1981) compared the "responsibility judgments" of students in the Just Community School and a similar alternative school, with those of students in conventional high schools. By dramatic margins, the two alternative schools' students were found to use "responsibility judgments" far more frequently than did their counterparts in regular high schools.

We interpret findings such as these as strong evidence that children will rise or fall to the level of expectation held out for them. In alternative schools, based on nurturing principles of child-raising, expectations are high. It is expected that children will want to learn, will want to be trustworthy, and will want to participate in a joyful, moral community. The absence of rules forces children to think. The framework of pro-social values encourages them to think responsibly.

In conventional schools, expectations are generally low. While rhetoric may exhort students to high levels of behavior, the systems they live by do just the opposite. When students are not responsible for their community, they are less likely to learn responsibility in it.

THE EFFECTS OF SCHOOLING ON EMPATHY

Empathy grows out of a sense of responsibility toward other people. This sense of responsibility is fostered best in schools that develop a positive social climate in which students feel an obligation to uphold the collective norms of the community. Nurturing schools have been shown to do this better than conventional schools.

A conventional school may have strong school spirit. But school spirit is not the same as a sense of community. School spirit often has an "us" versus "them" component. It often surfaces in the face of competition (as opposed to cooperation). It can be rooted in immoral or irresponsible behavior, such as hazing, vandalizing, or bad-mouthing an opponent. A sense of community, however, requires a common social goal. It is the sharing of *values* as opposed to the sharing of *victory*.

Students in conventional schools often display little awareness of community. Where collective norms do exist, they are often exclusive and antisocial in nature: *don't help out, don't rat on anybody, don't show enthusiasm for learning.* The best way to illustrate the dramatic differences in climate between conventional and nurturing schools is to listen to comments from students who attend them. The students were asked a question that we think zeroes in on the value a school places on responsibility and empathy: whether they and their peers should and would help others out in their school (Higgins et al., 1981).

Here are their responses. First, from students in the alternative schools:

> *Anyone who is [here] knows they should help out. . . .*
> *Why?*
> *Because [it] is a community. Because you have a responsibility to the kids in this school. You are supposed to think of them as part of the school and part of the community, so you should do it.*
> *It's . . . good to help people. It's an unwritten code that you do help people here. . . . People are here to work together . . . that's one of the reasons they came here. . . . The school functions well if people want to help each other out.*

In some respects we are just an enlarged family and I would trust everybody in my family. We work as a family, or as a team, or as a community. . . . Community is very important and it is more important than any kind of peer pressure.

Contrast the comments from students in conventional high schools:

I don't consider this school a community. Too many people hold grudges against each other, because maybe they look or act different. Or some kids come to school to be with their friends or to get stoned, and some kids come to do the work.

[The school] is very grouped with cliques. If you're outside the clique, they don't care about you. . . . They don't understand what life and helping people is all about.

I think this school really lacks . . . togetherness. Nobody really takes pride in school except a few who are good students or very good athletes. Where people don't take pride in something, go out of their way to help each other, the community doesn't really benefit. It doesn't promote the welfare of the school. . . . There is no sense of caring, helping each other.

Schools that succeed in promoting responsibility and empathy use community pride and peer pressure for the good of the group. The children themselves push each other to behave morally; in the same way that it may be "cool" in conventional schools to be laid back and uninvolved, it is "cool" in nurturing schools to be morally committed and to care. These students recognize that dishonest or insensitive acts threaten the community. This understanding and sense of belonging fosters the growth of empathy.

Our purpose here is not to indict teachers and administrators for conditions in American classrooms, although some, no doubt, are indictable. Nor is it to question how our society can allow its current decimation of school budgets, staffs, and programs, although such a question is critical to ask. Rather, it is to lay a foundation of understanding that will allow parents to find those teachers and schools that *do* value and nurture creativity, responsibility, and empathy.

CHECKLIST FOR SELECTING TEACHERS

The attributes on this checklist apply primarily to the individual teacher and classroom. Naturally, a teacher's ability to carry them out will be enhanced by supportive colleagues and administrators, and by a system-wide philosophy that encourages such methods and values. Even without this support, however, it is still possible for a teacher to run his or her classroom as an oasis of nurturing teaching and learning. This is particularly true in the elementary grades, where the classroom forms the basic community. Parents can seek out those teachers who value and nurture creativity, responsibility, and empathy, even if the larger school environment does not.

The following checklist is designed to be a creative tool for parents to use in selecting their children's teachers. You may wish to use it while observing in a particular teacher's classroom. If you see the teacher engage in a behavior on the list, place a checkmark next to it (discreetly, of course). The more checkmarks, the more likely the teacher is to reinforce your family's educational values. Another way to use this list is to give it to other parents and teachers, or even to the principal of your child's school. Tell them that these are the characteristics you wish your child's teachers to have. Solicit their recommendations. Request and/or observe for yourself those teachers whose names come up most frequently.

We have divided characteristics into those that support creativity, and those that support the growth of responsibility and empathy. Naturally, there is considerable overlap between the two.

Teacher Characteristics that Nurture Creativity

_____ Sets up the discovery process by encouraging students to initiate their own learning and to study independently.

At least some assignments offer students a wide range of opportunities for fulfilling them; students are allowed to modify the focus of work under progress in response to new information and interests.

___ Reinforces and sustains student perplexity.
The goal, of course, is not to keep students in a perpetual state of perplexity but to train them to better tolerate ambiguity. Teachers in a nurturing school use perplexity as a motivator of learning: "That *is* a mystery! But if you go on in your reading I think you'll find an answer." "Keep trying and I'm sure you'll discover why your experiment hasn't worked yet."

___ Rewards and redirects student questions back to the student.
"That's a good question, Jim. Can you guess what the answer might be?" "There's no doubt in my mind, Felicia, that a smart girl like you can figure that out all by herself!"

___ Refrains from being overly critical.
The teacher couches criticisms in terms that emphasize faulty *behavior* and not faulty children: "Billy, hitting hurts people and is not something we do in this class," as opposed to "Billy, only naughty boys hit their classmates." Critiques of student work are gentle and encouraging; strengths as well as weaknesses are enumerated.

___ Encourages free exchange of ideas.
"Class, how would you respond to Susan's question?" "Does anyone have a different idea?" "How would someone with the opposite point of view defend that position?" "You've all made some very interesting points." Discussions are held without the imperative of having to reach a conclusion or "right" answer.

___ Supports students in seeking evidence for their viewpoints.
"That's your opinion, and that's fine, Anne. But can you back it up?" "What information would you need to know, Tim, to confirm your theory?"

_____ Looks for quality over quantity in students' work.

"How long does it have to be?" is the perennial question students ask about written assignments. "No longer than you need to do the job well," the nurturing teacher is likely to respond. Nurturing teachers cultivate concise, sharply focused writing by sharing examples of such work aloud and pointing out how success was achieved.

_____ Rewards imaginative efforts.

As we have mentioned, payoffs for creativity are counterproductive. But many teachers seem to punish or ignore creativity through excessive concern for grammar, spelling, and so on. Nurturing teachers express delight when students take imaginative flyers, and will sometimes overlook faulty mechanics in order to stimulate motivation and intellectual growth.

_____ Uses a wide variety of teaching methods.

The nurturing teacher maintains a lively, unpredictable classroom. She avoids the ruts that take excitement and spontaneity out of learning. Look for a variety of assignment types (short-term, long-term, individual, group, written, verbal, qualitative, quantitative, library-based, experiential) and teaching methods (field trips, student presentations, debates, guest speakers, games, media, computer use, etcetera).

_____ Has a warm, friendly relationship with students.

Nurturing teachers take interest in the personal lives of their students and demonstrate age-appropriate physical and verbal affection. Students like to "hang out" with nurturing teachers; look for informal, "nonschool" conversations and groups of kids huddling around the teacher's desk.

_____ Refrains from being evaluative; encourages students to judge their work themselves.

"How do _you_ think you did?" "Where do you think you've improved?" "Where do you think you need to work harder?" This is not to say that the nurturing teacher never grades student work. Whenever a student is able to judge the adequacy of his own efforts, however, she seizes the chance to teach him to do so.

_____ Has many resources readily available within the classroom. As we have emphasized, children learn with all their senses, and love variety. Look for a plethora of resource materials readily available. Beware of too much order and neatness. If you see a lot of "seat work" being done on "work sheets" by every child in the class at once, watch out!

_____ Encourages questioning and is not shaken by unexpected questions.
Flexibility is a key trait of nurturing teachers—they rejoice in the unexpected responses of their students. Beware of irritability and rigidity in teacher reactions to student queries.

_____ Provides for student presentations and long-term projects. Both types of classwork require extra time, patience, and planning on the part of the teacher. With morale generally lower among America's educators these days, these teaching methods are harder to find.

_____ Models creativity in approach to classroom displays and environment.
An obvious tip-off to a teacher's personality and education philosophy is the organization of the classroom setting. A conventional layout (all the desks in a row; boring, yellowed pictures on the wall) will usually indicate a lack of creative imagination. Beware of stagnant environments. Look for changing displays and furniture arrangements, look for objects you wouldn't expect to find in a classroom, and especially, look for whimsy and signs that students and teachers have personalized the classroom to make it their own.

_____ Projects enthusiasm for learning.
Nurturing teachers do not see themselves as the font of all knowledge. They demonstrate an eagerness to learn from

their students, as well as *with* their students: "Let's see if we can find out together." "I never thought of looking at it that way!" They often have outside interests, which mark *them* as learners, that they share with their students.

____ Encourages intellectual and creative risk-taking.

"Wow, what an interesting theory! Let's see how you can check it out." "That idea didn't work, but look at all we've learned from trying to make it work!" "Imagine the courage it took to propose that the earth was round when everybody believed it was flat!" Look for brainstorming to generate ideas, assignments that push kids to develop their own hypotheses and explanations, and discussions that do not shy from difficult issues or extreme positions.

____ Takes a positive and supportive attitude toward student failure.

Some teachers see failure as totally bad, to be avoided at all costs. Nurturing teachers point out the pluses of failure. They offer emotional and practical support to students at times of frustration. Look to see if children learn *why* they failed; is failure an endpoint or a step in an ongoing process? Does the teacher go over tests and papers to be sure students understand and learn from errors?

____ Is able to knowledgeably discuss his or her views of the creative process with you.

Talk to your child's prospective teacher. Don't be afraid to interview him as you would any professional you are considering to do a job for you. Ask his attitude about the various points we have raised in this questionnaire, and if you don't like what you hear (and see), keep looking. It's your right. A nurturing teacher will never be offended by such questioning; he will value the concern you show for your child's education, and appreciate the respect your questions reflect upon his professionalism.

Teacher Characteristics that Nurture Responsibility and Empathy

____ Catches children being good.

"That was very thoughtful of you to help Susan with her work." "I was so proud when the substitute teacher told me that you were the best class she's ever taught." Nurturing teachers are on the lookout for behaviors they can reinforce. They use this technique rather than threatening or punishing. If possible, they simply ignore inappropriate behavior, because paying attention to it, even if only to scold, frequently reinforces it.

____ Sets up exercises in responsibility.

Students are given classroom jobs besides cleaning the erasers: tutoring, attendance taking, collecting money, organizing class projects, participating in decision-making, caring for classroom menageries, and so on. One teacher we know writes up lists of questions for books the children are expected to read. When one child finishes a book, she is "checked out" on the list by a child who has already read the book.

____ Rewards responsibility with greater privileges and autonomy.

Trustworthy students have greater choice in assignments, more freedom to leave the classroom or school grounds, and obvious leadership roles. In one school we know of, significant acts of responsibility are rewarded by being allowed to be the "principal's assistant" for an hour.

____ Communicates high expectations for student trustworthiness.

Many teachers anticipate misbehavior (and thus provide suggestions for how to do so): "I want no running around when we get there." "If anyone makes noise he will be sent to wait in the bus." Nurturing teachers assure children of their confidence in them: "I know you'll show Dr. Jones how much we appreciate her taking us through the laboratory."

_____ Shows interest in social and emotional needs of students. "Is your dad feeling better yet, Bob?" "How does your grandmother like her new job, Jenny?" "You seem a bit down these days, Ramon. Is everything okay?"

_____ Takes class time to deal with moral issues and problems. Rather than resolve ethical quandaries with edicts, nurturing teachers provide opportunities for students to discuss issues and propose solutions.

_____ Encourages initiative and helping out.
"Thank you for thinking of that. It totally slipped my mind!" "I really liked the way you showed Harry how to do that, Juan." "If Lynn gets tired, why don't we all take turns helping her." Look for an ethic of caring: class projects that help others, get-well cards to students who are ill, kids tutoring kids, and the like.

_____ Fosters warm, informal and multifaceted teacher-pupil interactions.
Relationships go beyond strict teacher-student role definitions. Teachers share interests and appropriate elements of their personal lives with students. "Nonschool" opportunities for interacting are provided: ice-skating, camping, ski trips, picnics, group cooking, and so forth.

_____ Listens attentively and respectfully to students' statements. Watch how the teacher handles such interactions. You can usually tell if she is putting on a performance for your benefit. Some teachers have an edge of sarcasm or disdain as they address their students. They may even occupy themselves with writing on the blackboard or turning pages in a book rather than give their full attention to the child speaking. Nurturing teachers use eye contact and body language (such as nodding one's head) to encourage communication.

_____ Provides opportunities for students to discuss and role-take issues of fairness and moral complexity.

Role-taking can mean that each participant in a conflict is asked to explain how the other feels, or to represent a particular person or point of view. Classroom incidents may be reenacted to allow children to "try on" various options for behavior.

____ Allows students to participate in decision-making that affects their interests.
Rules for classroom behavior, topics for study or discussion, the nature of assignments, the specifics for homework—all are subject to teacher-student negotiations.

____ Encourages students to propose solutions for classroom problems such as stealing, cheating, or hurting feelings.
Nurturing teachers recognize that students are much more likely to follow rules if they have had a hand in formulating them. Furthermore, they trust that children will consider such issues with wisdom and fairness.

____ Relates individual actions to community needs.
Classrooms are really miniature communities in which the actions of the one or the few can affect the many. Numerous lessons about appropriate civic behavior can be learned there, but only if the teacher is willing and able to point out the relationships between individual and group rights.

____ Bases authority on quality of teacher-student relationships and shared standards for appropriate behavior.
Nurturing teachers recognize that respect, caring, and mutually held values form the optimal basis for authority in the classroom. They seek voluntary cooperation from their students and try to refrain from having to invoke their authority as teachers.

____ Models concern for individual rights and feelings.
As we have reported, teachers tend to be authoritarian. They are likely, therefore, to believe that "rank has its privileges," and that students should do as they are ordered. Nurturing teachers tend to be much more egalitarian. This can be ob-

served from the classroom's organization as well as the way in which the teacher solicits and accepts student input.

____ Shows flexibility based on needs of individual children. Authoritarian teachers often believe that fairness dictates that all students be treated the same. It's also easier to do that. The nurturing teacher realizes that individuals are inherently different, and so fairness dictates a caring for individual needs. Beware of rigid rule structures and inviolate curricula. Look for assignments and resources that permit children to work at different rates and on different interests. Exceptions should be the rule.

In order to find these teachers, listen to the grapevine. Other parents whose children have gone before yours can offer valuable advice. Kids themselves often know who the best teachers are— and their criteria will intuitively be remarkably similar to yours. Visit your child's school. You have the right to meet with the principal, to observe, and to request certain teachers. As educators ourselves, we're certainly not suggesting that you be a pain in the cl-ass. But you can make your views known. Represent your interests as a parent, and your child's as a student, while still being supportive of school personnel. Let's face it, the school principal is much more likely to grant the requests of the parent sitting in his office, than the parent whom he or she has never met.

If you find a teacher who meets most of these criteria, you and your child are indeed fortunate. Ideally, though, one hopes to find teachers such as these in a school with a principal in a system with administrators in a community with a school board in a state with a legislature that *all* value creativity, responsibility, and empathy. (Good luck!) Toward that end, we include another checklist that addresses larger issues:

SCHOOL CHARACTERISTICS THAT NURTURE CREATIVITY, RESPONSIBILITY, AND EMPATHY

____ Has a written (and disseminated) statement of educational philosophy which values individual rights, intellectual freedom, social responsibility, and the creation of a moral, mutually supportive community.

____ Has goals that encompass social and emotional as well as academic development.

____ Is governed by participatory democracy.
Ideally, students and teachers have equal rights and votes. Policies are set in community meetings. Where this is not the case, students at least have meaningful opportunities for input; student governments have autonomy to deal with issues of larger import than soda machines and prom-night bands. For example, they have a voice in establishing disciplinary policies, curriculum opportunities, and evaluation methods.

____ Has a curriculum that is flexible and designed to adapt to individual student needs and interests.
For example, students might be able to satisfy a particular assignment by writing a paper, making a film, or presenting a lesson to the class. Look for independent study opportunities, multimedia availability, ongoing conferences between students and teachers, team-teaching, etcetera.

____ Has a curriculum that includes real-life issues involving questions of morality, justice, and responsibility.

____ Offers opportunities for field trips, apprenticeships, and other hands-on, off-campus learning.

____ Has identifiable incentives to motivate responsibility and pro-social behavior, such as leadership roles, increased freedom, options, and privileges.

____ Allows teachers a high degree of autonomy in areas of curriculum development. Encourages them to build deep and broadly based relationships with students.

_____ Responds to crises and tragedies with sensitivity and meaningful programs.

_____ Demonstrates institutional social conscience in its relation to larger societal, environmental, and global issues (such as recycling, racism, world hunger, the homeless).

_____ Encourages androgyny; all classes and activities are available to children of both genders.

_____ Has mentor programs and cross-age tutoring.

_____ Engenders pride and respect from students, parents, teachers, and administrators.

"Dream on," you say. "If such a school exists, let us know. We'll all move there!" Such schools *do* exist.

Research suggests that private schools possess more of the characteristics associated with the fostering of responsibility and empathy than do conventional public schools. This may stem from such a school's sense of purpose and community, small classes, close student-teacher relationships, and high expectations for student performance. It would be a mistake, however, to conclude that the issue is one of public versus private schooling. Educator Donald Erickson (1981) found that while it is true that private schools are most effective in creating the type of social climate identified with positive moral development, it is not privateness, per se, that makes these schools effective. Rather:

The most effective schools are distinguished, not by elaborate facilities, extensively trained teachers, small classes, or high levels of financial support, but by outstanding social climates.

In having to "sell" a product, private schools have had to make a statement about their values and traditions, their morals and goals. This draws together parents, students, and teachers who *choose* to share and identify with these definitions. What creates this superior climate is:

... [that] kind of cohesive community or "fellowship" that exists when people are held together by mutual commitment to common purposes and to each other, by a sense of doing something special, and by consensus about the goals to be achieved, and by congruence of values between home and school (Erickson, 1982).

In the past, public schools have not had to sell their wares, and thus have not had to be particularly concerned with the type of school climate they create (although given the current political climate, this may be changing). There are, however, many public schools that *do* meet our criteria for fostering creativity, responsibility, and empathy. Some of these are "traditional" schools that sparkle with the social and educational values of a creative, charismatic principal—one who is able to inspire a special atmosphere of purpose, respect, and belonging—motivating students and teachers to high levels of achievement and commitment. Other public school systems contain a "school-within-a-school" which operates according to the values we have discussed. These alternative programs have been shown to be more successful than conventional ones in fostering community values, in motivating moral behavior, and in helping students to feel capable and successful. Students who attend these alternative public schools express dramatically higher levels of satisfaction than do their regular-program peers.

According to research, the organization of a social system influences behavior. Parents recognize this in the social systems they create within their family. In searching for a school that will reinforce the values of their home and foster responsibility and empathy, nurturing parents must seek schools that are highly moral in their structures, values, and human relationships. John Dewey (1975) offers a definition of these schools:

In so far as the school represents, in its own spirit, a genuine community life; in so far as what are called school discipline, government, order, etc., are the expression of this inherent social spirit; in so far as the methods used are those that appeal to the active and constructive powers, permitting the child to give out and thus to serve; in so far as the curriculum is so selected and organized as to provide the material for affording the child a consciousness of the world in which he has to play a part, and the demands he has to meet; so far as these ends are met, the school is organized on an ethical basis.

You may wonder what our own study revealed about the relationship between creativity and schools. Based on what we have said in this chapter, one would assume that we found strong associations between creativity and the type of school the children attended. We did not. There was no correlation between the children's creativity ratings and the innovativeness of their school. In fact, the parents and children in our study agreed that their schools had little, if any, effect on creativity.

We know, however, that schools *do* affect creativity. Researchers have a considerable body of evidence suggesting causal relationships between a school's social climate and educational philosophy, and its students' behavior and attitudes.

Why then, did schools not surface in our study as critical to creative growth? There are several likely reasons for this paradox:

1.   Nurturing parents compensate for the effects of a nonnurturing school on their children's creativity, negating its influence. Thus, those children in our study who attended "bad" schools were able to remain highly creative in spite of their school environment.

2.   Only parents who already value creativity are likely to enroll their child in an innovative school. Thus, those children in our study who went to alternative schools were already operating at high levels of creativity by dint of their home environment. Attendance at such schools would be the educational equivalent of bringing coals to Newcastle, and would not have a significant effect on already high creativity ratings.

3.   Our research did not address the effects of highly nurturing schools on children raised in home environments of low or average creativity. This is where one would expect to find evidence of the positive effects the right school can have on creative ability.

We have spoken about the effects of school on the personality traits fostered by nurturing parenting. We have not, however, considered the effects of these personality traits on a child's schoolwork. What is the relationship between, say, a preference for disorder and being able to do well in school, or between creative ability and good study habits?

There is no question that pristine school notebooks and conscientious study habits foster the type of learning and achievement valued in most schools. They do not, however, foster creativity; they can, in fact, inhibit it. The skills that support high academic achievement—good note-taking, rote memorization, organization, being able to guess what will be asked on the exam—are usually not relevant to creative growth. Similarly, the personality traits linked to creativity—preference for disorder, tolerance of ambiguity, risk-taking—can be at odds with the narrow "right answer" approach to learning which exists in most schools. Creativity frequently shatters convention. Those who push at the boundaries may not receive A's from those hired to pass tradition along. Similarly, because the kids in our study have developed a sense of responsibility and empathy, they are especially alert to the injustices and inconsistencies that abound in most school environments. The child who challenges school personnel over issues of authority or fairness is not likely to endear herself to the powers that be.

We know that poorer school performance has been associated with authoritarian and permissive parenting styles. But what do we know about the effects of nurturing parenting? A recent study (Grolnick and Ryan, 1989) examined parenting styles associated with children's self-regulation and competence in school. The researchers found that parental *autonomy support* was most consistently and positively related to children's self-regulation and competence, as measured through children's self-reports, teacher ratings, and standardized tests. *Autonomy support* was defined by the researchers as ". . . the degree to which parents value and use techniques which encourage independent problem solving, choice, and participation in decisions versus externally dictating outcomes, and motivating achievement through punitive disciplinary techniques, pressure or controlling rewards." Thus this study reveals that children raised with a high degree of autonomy support have the highest grades and achievement, are most competent, and are assessed by their teachers to have the fewest behavior problems. This, of course, is good news to nurturing parents since autonomy support is a critical part of their approach to child-raising.

One personality trait that did come up frequently in our discussions with parents around the topic of school performance was preference for disorder. As one parent in our study put it, "I am totally mystified how my child manages to do so well in school. You know that character in 'Peanuts,' the one who goes around in a cloud of dirt? My child seem to go around in a perpetual cloud of disorganization. But someplace, internally, he must have it together because he still does fine in school." This boy is typical of highly creative kids; his "order" is idiosyncratic and invisible to the outside world. But it exists just as concretely for him as do file folders and index cards for the next person.

Our advice to parents about disorder and schoolwork is this: if your kids are doing fine, leave them alone. No matter how messy their notebook or illegible their handwriting, if it ain't broke, don't fix it.

For other kids, there is no internal coherence hiding behind their disorganized notebooks, lost assignment papers, and misplaced materials. In order to do well in school, these kids will have to surmount their disordered work habits. Parents can help by explaining how much easier good study skills can make things. They can show their child how to organize a notebook, how to take notes, how to identify the major points in a chapter, how to study for a test, how to break assignments into manageable chunks, how to schedule time. It's extraordinary, but most schools never teach children how to do any of this. There is no reason for a child to do poorly in school simply for lack of having learned how to do well. School is too important an arena for the development of a child's self-confidence and social comfort.

We noticed something else about nurturing parents. They talk to their children about school. Not "How was school today?" and "Have you done your homework?" and "What grade did you get on your test?" No, they talk about the beliefs and purposes of their children's school—and how its methods relate to family values. Nurturing parents help their children to form honorable and constructive relationships with their schools by discussing with them *why* their teachers are acting as they are, and what their children should do in turn. They discuss the assumptions behind school policies and assignments. "Why do you think they make you study chemistry?" "If you were the principal, how would you deal with this problem?" "Have you thought of telling the teacher how you feel?" Sometimes these discussions lead to the parents siding with their child against the teacher or school policy.

Some parents have expressed the worry to us that criticism of their children's school or teachers will undermine their children's performance or already tenuous respect for the institution. Quite the contrary. Parental honesty will support the child by validating her sense of reality. Kids often just need a parent to say, "I know it's hard. I know it's unfair. I know it's dumb, but, hey, you've just got to hang in there."

It's important to keep in mind that doing well in school does not in and of itself create happiness, fine relationships, job satisfaction, intelligence, or creativity. Doing well in school allows one to continue to do well in more schools—at which point certain tickets are obtainable for various societal destinations. This is a valid reason that kids can and need to accept for learning to master the school environment. When presented to kids in this light, however, it allows them to keep their sense of self-worth separate from their school performance. It allows them to place a frame around the standards and values of the institution they attend—and even honor them—without losing their own. While A's and good study habits will serve a kid well for the next report card, the full spectrum of traits available to the nurtured child will serve him well for life.

Cultivating the "full spectrum of traits" described in this book is a tall order for any parent, even under the best of conditions. It cannot be achieved in an hour or two of "quality time" per week. However, as the lives of the children we studied make so evident, the results are *well worth it*. We sincerely hope this book will prove helpful to you in the most admirable quest to be a nurturing parent.

BIBLIOGRAPHY

Adorno, T. W., & others. 1950. *The Authoritarian Personality*. New York: Harper.

Amabile, T. 1989. *Growing Up Creative*. New York: Crown.

Amato, P. R. 1989. "Family processes and the competence of adolescents and primary school children." *Journal of Youth and Adolescence*. 18, (1) 39–53.

Baumrind, D. 1971. "Current patterns of parental authority." *Developmental Psychology Monographs*. 4, 1–103.

Bernstein, I. and Glenn, J. 1988. "The child and adolescent analyst's emotional reactions to his patients and their parents." *International Review of Psycho Analysis*. 43, (2) 225–241.

Collier, R. G., Jacobson, M. G., and Stahl, S. A. 1987. "Locus of control measurements for gifted and nongifted children." *Roeper Review,* 9, (3) 196–200.

Dacey, J. 1989. *Fundamentals of Creative Thinking*. Lexington, MA: Lexington Books/D.C. Heath.

Dacey, J. S., & Ripple, R. E. 1967. "The facilitation of problem solving and verbal creativity." *Psychology in the Schools*. 4, (3), 240–245.

deBono, E. 1984. "Empirically based treatment for parent-adolescent conflict." *Social Casework*. 65, (8) 487–495.

Dewey, J. 1975. *Moral Principles in Education*. Carbondale, IL: Southern Illinois University Press.

Duke, D. & Perry, C. 1978. "Can alternative schools succeed where Benjamin Spock, Spiro Agnew, and B. F. Skinner have failed?" *Adolescence*. 51, 375–392.

Duncker, K. 1945. "On problem solving." Trans. by Lees, L. S. *Psychological Monographs*. 58.

Elkind, D. 1987. *Mis-education: Preschoolers at Risk*. New York: Knopf.

Erickson, D. 1981. "A new strategy for school improvement." *Momentum*. December.

Erickson, D. 1982. *The British Columbia Story: Antecedents and Consequences of Aid to Private Schools*. Los Angeles, CA: Institute for the Study of Private Schools.

Flanagan, J. C. 1958. "Definition and measurement of ingenuity." In Taylor, C. W. (Ed.). *Second Utah Conference*.

Getzels, J. W. 1975. "Creativity." In Taylor, I. A. & Getzels, J. W., (Eds.). *Perspectives in Creativity*. Chicago: Aldine.

Gibran, K. 1973. *The Prophet*. New York: Knopf.

Grolnick, W. E. and Ryan, R. M. 1989. Parent styles associated with children's self-regulation and competence in school." *Journal of Educational Psychology*. 81, 143–154.

Hall, J. A. 1984. "Empirically based treatment for parent-adolescent conflict." *Social Casework*. 65, (8) 487–495.

Hallman, R. 1967. "Techniques of creative teaching." *Journal of Creative Behavior*. 1, (3), 325–330

Hamilton, S. F. and Fenzel, L. M. 1988. "The impact of volunteer experience on adolescent social development: Evidence of program effects." *Journal of Adolescent Research*. 3, (1) 65–80.

Helson, R. & Crutchfield, R. 1970. "Mathematicians." *Journal of Consulting and Clinical Psychology*. 34, 250–257.

Higgins, A., Power, C., and Kohlberg, A. 1981. "Student judgments of responsibility and the moral atmosphere of high schools: A comparative study." *Paper presented at the International Conference on Morality and Moral Development*. Miami Beach, FL. December 18, 1981.

Keltikangas, J. 1990. "Attributional style of the mother as a predictor of aggressive behavior of the child." *Aggressive Behavior*. 16, (1) 1–7.

Knowska, H. 1987. "Ksztalcenie empatii w szkole"/"Learning empathy in school." *Psychologia-Wychowawcza*. 30, (1) 81–86.

Kohlberg, L. & others. 1975. "The Just Community School: The theory and the Cambridge Cluster School experiment." In *Collected Papers from the Center for Moral Education*. Chapter 29, 3–39.

Levey, H. B. in Parnes, S. J. & Harding, H. F. (Eds.). 1962. *Source Book for Creative Thinking*. New York: Scribner's.

Luchins, A. S. 1952. "Mechanization in problem solving." *Psychological Monographs*. 54, (6).

MacKinnon, D. W. 1978. *In search of Human Effectiveness*. Buffalo, NY: Creative Education Foundation.

Mednick, S. A. 1963. "Research creativity in psychology graduate students." *Journal of Consulting Psychology*. 27, (3), 265–266.

Ortman, P. E. 1988. "Adolescents' perceptions of and feelings about control and responsibility in their lives." *Adolescence*. 23, (92) 913–924.

Osborn, A. 1963. *Applied Imagination*. New York: Scribner's.

Roe, A. (See Dacey, J., [1989] above for several references.)

Torrance, E. P. 1982. "Can we teach children to think creatively?" *Journal of Creative Behavior*. 6, (2), 114–143.

INDEX

A

Abuse of belongings, 107, 108
Accusative framing of problem, 170–71
Activities
  for androgyny traits
    goals of, 125
    Jack and Jill in the Box, 126–27
    other, 127–30
    Stop That Stereotyping, 125–26
  for balanced brain
    Give Yourself a Hand, 96–97
    Know Your Orange, 95–96
    Orienteering, 97–98
    other, 98–100
  for delay gratification ability
    Leaving One Stone Unturned, 84
    A Picnic of Sound, 86
    Shoe Box Collections, 85–86
    Time in the Bottle, 83–84
    Waiting for Good Dough, 86
    Wait and See(d), 85
    Write to the Source, 83
  for functional freedom traits
    Critter Training, 55–56
    How Am I Supposed to Paint Without a Paintbrush!, 56–57
    How Many Uses?, 56
    other, 59–60
    The Plants Are Dyeing!, 57–58
    Reinventing the Wheel, 58
  for originality traits
    Building Your Own Nest, 113–14
    other, 114–17
  for passion
    The Case of the Schoolyard Junk, 147–48
    Don't Be a Wet Blanket, 148–49
    other, 149–51
  for problem-solving ability
    Make a Hypothesis, 182–83
    other, 183–84

Sorting Shapes, 181–82
    Who Can Find the Raisin?, 180–81
  for self-control
    Create Your Own World, 142
    Get a Grip On Yourself!, 139–40
    Kim's Game, 138–39
    Now Playing On Your Neighborhood Mind!, 138
    other, 142–43
    Stop Thinking That!, 140–42
  for stimulus freedom traits
    The Alphabet People, 73–74
    Black Magic, 72–73
    Dream On, 74–75
    other, 75–76
  for tolerance of ambiguity, 164–66
Agitation, 133
Alphabet People, The, 73–74
Alternative schools. See Nurturing schools
Ambiguity, 152–53. See also Tolerance of ambiguity
Androgyny
  activities for fostering
    goals of, 125
    Jack and Jill in the Box, 126–27
    other, 127–30
    Stop That Stereotyping, 125–26
  characteristics of, 119–20
  creativity and, 118–19
  gender-role stereotyping and, 121–23
  nurturing parenting and, 123–24
  originality and, 112–13
  parents' background and, 120–21
  sexual orientation and, 124
Authoritarianism test, 190
Authoritarian parenting, 15, 156
Authoritative parenting, 16–17, 156
Autonomy, 38–39, 40. See also Respect
  support for, 210–11

activities for nurturing
  The Case of the Schoolyard Junk,
    147–48
  Don't Be a Wet Blanket, 148–49
  other, 149–51
  encouraging, 146–47
  occurrences of, 144–46
  and a plan, 134–35
Permissive parenting, 15–16, 156
Personality
  control of environment and, 107
  creativity and, 22
  delay gratification and, 77
  empathy and, 22
  fear of failure and, 65
  formation of, 13
  gender-role identity and, 119
  healthy, 22
  responsibility and, 22
  schooling and, 20
  success in life and, 22
Picnic of Sound, A, 86
Plan
  choosing and implementing,
    178–79
  passion and a, 134–35
Plants Are Dyeing!, The, 57–58
Positive consequences, 156
Praise, 39–42
Problems. See also Problem-solving
  accusative framing of, 170–71
  nonaccusative framing of, 170–71
  recognizing and defining, 168–71
  with schooling, 185–86
  symptoms and, 171
Problem-solving
  activities for nurturing
    Make a Hypothesis, 182–83
    other, 183–84
    Sorting Shapes, 181–82
    Who Can Find the Raisin?, 180–81
  functional fixity and, 55
  models of, 167–68
  natural, 167
  steps in
    analyzing options, 177–78
    choosing and implementing a
      plan, 178–79
    failures of, 179–80
    generating possible solutions,
      171–76

overview of, 168
recognizing and defining problem, 168–71
Protection, 18, 46–49
Public schools. See Conventional
  schools
Punishment, 108–10

R
Reflective listening, 37
Reinventing the Wheel, 58
Relationships, maintaining, 45
Relaxation, 133–34
Remote Associates Test, 104–5
Remote associations, 104–5
Respect, nurturing parenting and, 18,
  38–39
Responsibility
  characteristics of, 23
  conventional schools and, 191–92
  creativity and, 30
  delay gratification and, 80
  disorder and, 107
  empathy and, 25–26, 195
  nurturing schools and, 192–94
  personality and, 22
  school characteristics that nurture,
    205–9
  schooling and, 191–94
  teacher characteristics that nurture,
    202–5
Rewards, 42–43
Right-handedness, 89, 94–95
Right hemisphere of brain, 87, 89–90,
  91–92
Risk-taking
  authoritarian parenting and, 156
  authoritative parenting and, 156
  capacity, 155–56
  fear and, 158–60
  healthy level of, 155
  high, 160–62
  low, 158–60
  negative consequences and, 156
  nurturing parenting and, 156–58
  parents' feelings toward, 162–64
  permissive parenting and, 156
  positive consequences and, 156
  stimulus freedom and, 66
  tolerance of ambiguity and,
    154–58